GROW
HOUSE PLANTS
in temperate and cool climates

GROWING HOUSE PLANTS
in temperate and cool climates

Ross James

Lothian Publishing Company Pty Ltd
Melbourne Sydney Auckland

Acknowledgements

My thanks to Graeme Purdy and John Clasper of *Your Garden* magazine; Kevin Boyle and Pam Roseman of the *Weekly Times*; and Peter Brown of *Australian Horticulture* for their assistance and photographs used in this book.

First published 1987 by
Lothian Publishing Company Pty Ltd
11 Munro Street Port Melbourne Victoria 3207

National Library of Australia
Cataloguing-in-Publication data:

James, Ross.
  Growing house plants.

  Includes index.
  ISBN 0 85091 287 3.

  1. House plants. 2. Indoor gardening. I. Title.

635.9'65

Designed by Marius Foley
Typeset in Bembo & Helvetica by Bookset Pty Ltd
Printed in Singapore by Kyodo-Shing Loong Printing Industries Pte Ltd

CONTENTS

INTRODUCTION

THIS BOOK is designed to help you grow house plants successfully in temperate and cool climates. There is no doubt that house plants make both homes and work places more pleasant. They help to brighten and soften, and add beauty and colour to the surroundings. For those living in situations where a garden is impossible, house plants can provide much appreciated colour and greenery indoors.

Modern buildings, with their accent on better light and climate control, are ideal places to grow the wide range of plants suited to indoor culture. Many house plants are quite adaptable, so for those places with less than ideal light and temperature levels, there are plenty of plants to choose from.

Understanding your household environment is as important as knowing the cultural needs of the plant. No amount of advice will substitute for personal knowledge and observation.

The important areas of plant care, including watering, feeding, repotting, propagation, and pests and diseases, are discussed in general as well as within the plant description lists. Sections on ferneries, greenhouses, hanging baskets and terrariums are also included.

Some house plants are described in detail. These are excellent plants in cooler climates. Other plants, although still noteworthy, have been discussed in less detail. Flowering or foliage plants have been listed separately as each group has particular requirements. Special features such as flowering times, fragrance, light, heat and water requirements, and methods of propagation are listed in chart form, and a guide to the ailing plant is included for quick reference.

House plants can be grown by everyone. I hope this book will further your enjoyment and encourage you to use the many new and different plants available for household decoration.

Part 1

CARE AND CULTIVATION OF HOUSE PLANTS

SELECTING HOUSE PLANTS

HOUSE PLANTS are now so much an element of the household that their origin as outdoor plants is often forgotten. True, many are well adapted to a domestic life, but there are a proportion that should be considered only as temporary residents. The plant descriptions included in this book reflect the diversity of climates covered by commonly used house plants. This indirectly indicates their suitability for long- or short-term residency indoors.

An understanding that not all house plants appreciate the 'blanket treatment' approach or are suited to indoor culture permanently is necessary for success. Rules for plant care may be bent or broken to advantage on occasions, but in all fairness to the plant and to the grower, the advice given is best followed. Cyclamen, for example, flower during autumn and winter and grow naturally in areas of low humidity and clear crisp air. Recommendations generally given are for a cool, well-lit and preferably airy situation, and an even moisture level. Heated or stuffy rooms with air-conditioning are lethal and plant failure is rapid. The result is both predictable and avoidable by following the recommendations.

UNDERSTANDING YOUR HOME

Before choosing a house plant, you have first to be familiar with the light and temperature fluctuations within your home. Some plants have quite specific requirements; others are more adaptable.

Light

Flowering pot plants need plenty of bright light for the buds and flowers to reach full potential. Under poor light, petals may fade quickly and the buds drop off or fail to open. Foliage plants generally tolerate lower light levels and thus adapt to a wider selection of sites. In general those foliage plants with darkish foliage grow in poorly lit areas, and plants with highly coloured or variegated foliage require plenty of bright filtered light for strong growth and good leaf colour. The Aglaonemas (Chinese lucky plants) and *Philodendron cordatum* for example, grow well in poorly lit areas, while the brightly coloured *Codiaeum* (Croton) and *Dieffenbachia* revel in exceptionally bright conditions.

Temperature

Most homes have some form of heating. Different systems are kinder to plants than others. Oil and gas, and wood to a lesser degree, dry out the atmosphere noticeably, while electric floor heating and hot-water radiators cause less plant fatigue. Plants should stand well clear of all heat sources, especially hot-water radiators, pot-belly stoves and central-heating outlets. The concentrated energy from these is damaging to all plants, including those with the thickest and toughest leaves, and is positively disastrous for the delicate fronds of the maidenhair fern.

Heating is not essential for growing all house plants, but with heating some of the more exotic plant varieties can be grown. On the other hand, many winter-flowering pot plants dislike high temperatures and deteriorate quickly. *Cyclamen*, Polyanthus, *Calceolaria* and Cineraria prefer unheated rooms.

A PURCHASER'S GUIDE

Choosing a healthy plant is the first step in successful growing. You should look for:
- a balanced placement of foliage without gaps on specimen plants and fullness on multistem or bushy types;
- an absence of insect pests and disease;
- no yellow leaves or aborting flower buds;
- strong flower stems and plenty of buds;
- no stem damage caused by tying plants too tightly.

Price and quality

Plants are excellent value for the pleasure and beauty they give. Buying correctly at the outset can save a lot of disappointment and money. Plant prices reflect the time

they took to grow, the difficulty of culture, their rarity
and the quality of the final product. The better the quality, the higher the cost of production. Certainly, good
bargains do exist and it should not be assumed that cheap
plants are unhealthy. But be wary of those 'cheapies'
which have suffered a deterioration in quality as they
often fail to live up to expectations.

Labels

The directions on the plant label are necessarily brief.
Your local nursery has trained staff to provide extra
information on the requirements of a particular plant.
You should make a point of asking about the cultural
needs of each plant before purchasing it.

HOUSE LIFE

Sadly, plants have set lifetimes in the wild, and their
service as domestics does nothing to delay the in-built
time-clock. The artificiality of household cultivation
shortens this lifetime somewhat, but this should not
discourage their use.

The annual varieties, the source of seasonal colour, are
invaluable for splashes of brightness throughout the gardening calendar both in and out of doors. One common
method is to plant up a number of containers and swap
them over, week by week. One week's fatigue is easier to
counteract than 4 weeks in one spell. Keep in mind that
they add temporary colour and don't hesitate to replace
them with fresh plants once their peak has been reached.
Among the suggested varieties are Cineraria, *Coleus*,
Schizanthus, *Calceolaria* and *Primula*.

There are those flowering house plants which live longer indoors than others and are an ideal substitute for cut
flowers. The African violet (and related gesneriads),
Anthurium, chrysanthemums, *Kalanchoe*, poinsettia, and
the Rieger begonias fulfil this role admirably.

Unlike so many of the flowering varieties which are
naturally short-lived, foliage house plants have a longer
life. The family heirloom of an *Aspidistra* or a kentia palm
is common enough and the botanical gardens of the
world have advanced specimens in continuous cultivation dating from the 1880s. This is not to say that all
foliage house plants last forever — they have different
lifetimes which are shortened by incorrect culture.

WATERING

THE ONE aspect of indoor gardening that causes so much heartache and indecision is watering. You may have already killed the odd plant by being heavy-handed with the water. Unfortunately it is impossible to set out hard and fast rules for each and every plant because of the differences between homes, the pots and potting mixtures, the seasons and the plants themselves.

THE ROOT SYSTEM

Plants have two parts to their root system — the basic framework which penetrates the soil and anchors the plant, and the fine root-hair network which absorbs the water and minerals needed to sustain growth. The root hairs are only produced immediately behind the tip of the root. As each section of root matures, the root hairs disappear and are not replaced. Thus the plant needs a healthy and active root system to flourish.

Roots need oxygen from the air to function and die if the supply is inadequate. Soil comprises components of many sizes interspersed with water and pockets of air. In a waterlogged soil the air (containing oxygen) is replaced by water and the fine root hairs soon die. Such conditions are also conducive to the root-rotting fungi which are quick to infect stressed roots, thus cutting off a large proportion of the water and food supply. So it is that a plant which grows in moist (wet) soil continually wilts, yet fails to respond to additional water. Once root rot sets in, complete recovery is rarely successful and it is better to discard the plant and start again.

In comparison, a dry soil has too much air and not enough water for roots to survive. Roots in dry soil gradually shrivel and die. However, the basic framework remains healthy and sound and new feeder roots arc produced once the moisture level is satisfactory.

TYPE OF PLANT

The summertime water requirement of all plants is higher than the winter requirement, and even then allowances for individual differences must be made. The piggy-back plant (*Tolmeia menziesii*) is an exceptionally thirsty plant, needing even moisture at all times. On the other hand, the snake plant (*Sansevieria*) uses much less water and should be kept dryish over winter to prevent rotting, and kept only moderately moist during summertime. You cannot hope to succeed by watering a piggy-back plant in the same way as a snake plant, and vice versa.

This croton has been under-watered with the resultant leaf drop, and growth has ceased.

Hence, for many plants, an all-at-once approach will ensure a short and disappointing life. The timing of watering must always recognize how much a plant's needs change throughout the year, rather than giving regular set amounts irrespective of growth.

LIGHT AND TEMPERATURE

Housing styles and structural materials are many and varied. Both have an important bearing on the light and temperature levels within. Even light levels in homes with plenty of window space may be poor because of the shadowing effect of adjoining buildings and nearby greenery.

In the main, cool-climate growers get best results from the east to westerly aspects. Southerly aspects rarely provide sufficient light for good growth all year round. Consider the watering regimes needed for two different species, one plant of each growing in two rooms identical except for their orientation. The plants are the *Sansevieria* and the *Tolmeia*, and they are located in a north-facing room and a south-facing room. Both rooms are unheated. Throughout the year the watering consumption will vary noticeably and may be as follows

Piggy-back plant *(Tolmeia menziesii)*

Season	North room	South room
Summer months	4 times weekly	2 times weekly
Winter months	2 times weekly	once weekly

Snake plant *(Sansevieria)*

Season	North room	South room
Summer months	once per week	once every 3 weeks
Winter months	once per 2 weeks	once per 6 to 8 weeks

The difference in water usage for each plant can be attributed to aspect — the extra amount of light and heat the north-facing room receives would increase water requirements. The water needs of each species are also markedly different, as discussed earlier.

Daylight and daylength is at a peak during summer, nonetheless because the sun is lower in the sky during winter the light levels in rooms which face north may be such that plants continue to grow vigorously and the reduction in water use is not as marked as you would expect. Plants growing in east and west-facing rooms usually require less water over the winter than during the summer period.

HEATING AND COOLING

It is easy to overlook the importance of heaters and coolers in influencing plant performance. Certainly heaters permit slightly less hardy species to thrive in cooler climates. Whether or not growth continues throughout the cooler months depends primarily upon adequate light, heat being less important. Plants growing in well-lit conditions with normal room heating require more water than those in unheated rooms. On the other hand, evaporative cooling (which adds moisture to the air) reduces heat stress and so cuts down on the amount of water plants transpire during hot weather, and so reduces the frequency of watering.

THE POTTING MEDIUM

The mix in which plants grow is as important to plant health and growth as the surroundings. The frequency of watering also depends on the mixture and its ability to retain and release the moisture. The initial composition dictates to a large extent how the mix will perform as the plant grows and uses it. A mix with a high clay and high organic matter content usually means less watering than one with the opposite characteristics. If your compost is clay-based, the drainage may deteriorate in time as the organic material decomposes, whereas a compost that is well-drained at the outset usually remains so and, in fact, may become more porous as it is further aerated by the roots. Beware, however, of assuming that sandy mixtures drain well. Those incorporating plenty of fine sand may well end up no better than the clay-based type. The fine sand fills in the spaces between the coarse particles in much the same way as it does in concrete.

Most nurseries have their own mixtures which often have different drainage characteristics. It is helpful to pay particular attention until you have determined the type of mix used. Sometimes I find it is more satisfactory to repot the plant into a mix that I know.

THE POT

The choice of container — porous or non-porous — does alter watering frequency. The old-fashioned, unglazed terracotta pot is porous, which means that water evaporates from the pot surface. This leads to a faster and more even drying-out of the potting mixture.

Non-porous containers, which include ceramics, plastics or glazed terracotta, do not lose water from their surface, and hence dry out less evenly and need less frequent watering.

If the surface of the soil is dry in a porous pot, then the entire soil ball is dry and watering is needed. In a non-porous container, the soil in the lower half of the pot may still be moist enough even though the surface is dry.

Pot size also influences the frequency of watering. Consider the two piggy-back plants again, this time in the same room. One is in a 10 cm pot, the other in a 15 cm pot. Clearly the simple difference of the volume of the potting mixture — threefold in this instance — means less frequent watering for the larger pot. Repotting to a larger size is recommended should a plant require daily watering.

HOW AND WHEN TO WATER

The methods for determining when to water are varied and as such often include a number of unspoken quirks that get lost in the telling. They include such gems as tapping the pot, the dryness of the surface soil, today is Tuesday (and therefore watering day), and probing the soil with the index finger. Regrettably very few of these and the many variations on them take account of the factors discussed earlier in this chapter. A quick review of these, in order, is:

- type of plant;
- home/office climate;
- type and age of potting mixture;
- type and size of pot;
- personal knowledge and observation.

Juggling all these is not as difficult as it seems if the following method is adopted. It is based on the weight of the plant, pot and potting mix both when dryish and when wet. For example, a dry piggy-back plant in a 15 cm pot weighs 500 g. Water is added and the excess drains away. The pot and plant now weigh 650 g — any increase in weight is water. At the same time the state of the soil surface is noted — it is usually lighter in colour when dry. But remember that the soil in non-porous containers may be quite dry on the surface but damp to wet at the base of the pot.

After your next watering, check each plant daily by lifting the pot to 'feel' the weight, and note the soil colour. As the moisture content diminishes the pot will 'feel' lighter and the soil colour will alter. By repeating the routine two to three times — especially for any new plants — it soon becomes possible to glance at the soil surface for an accurate indication of watering needs. If in doubt, lift the pot to confirm the diagnosis. Understandably the larger sized pots are impractical, if not impossible, to treat in this way.

Soil moisture meters certainly assist where containers are not too deep. These have a long probe which is pushed into the soil and gives a reading of how much moisture is in the soil and if watering is necessary. While they are a useful guide, they are no substitute for learning how to water each plant. This comes only with direct experience.

Warm water is essential for the majority of tropical varieties during winter to prevent chilling of the root system. Cold, wet soil causes far greater problems than low room temperatures. A good rule is to use warm water at all times because, as well as helping prevent chilling, it assists in moistening dry soil and helps flush out fertilizer salts.

To ensure thorough watering, pots must be filled to the brim and the excess water should drain through the holes at the base. Very dry soil, which tends to repel moisture, may require additional topping up or you may prefer to plunge the pot into warm water. This should not be done regularly because many of the finer-rooted varieties will suffer, e.g. *Saintpaulia*, *Begonia*, *Peperomia* and *Pilea*.

Of course plants have ways of showing thirst and these are additional indicators. Some signs are:
- a dulling or greying of leaf colour and gloss;
- wilting and yellowing foliage;
- premature flower and leaf loss;
- overall limpness.

A special note: these signs of dryness also indicate water-logging which causes root death. In both cases the plant cannot get sufficient moisture. The 'lifting' test referred to earlier is valuable to determine the moisture content of the growing mix.

Thus, when determining when to water, remember:
- to treat each plant according to its needs;
- to use warm water;
- to water thoroughly;
- to keep the plant slightly drier in unheated or cool rooms;
- not to leave plants sitting in water;
- that personal experience is your teacher.

FEEDING

WHILE PLANTS have the ability to manufacture their own food, they need an adequate supply of raw materials to do so. These raw materials include carbon, hydrogen, oxygen and an assortment of essential and minor elements.

You must remember that the plant grown in a pot is in a different situation to the plant in the garden. It depends totally upon your assistance for survival and cannot reap the benefits of any composting of the garden or additions to the soil by way of rainfall or plant and animal by-products. In the pot, the roots mine the potting mixture and extract the available nutrients for building into plant tissue. Unless these nutrients are replaced, the mixture becomes deficient which then affects the plant by degrees until satisfactory growth stops.

Mountains of soft lush foliage is not necessarily indicative of a healthy plant. Balance is the operative word, which means that the object of feeding is to keep the plant in sound health by providing the right amount of fertilizer at the right time. The approach of 'A little, often, is better than a lot at once' works very well. This means weak doses frequently instead of one or two large (over) doses. By adopting this course, growth is nudged along gently and has the strength and vigour to withstand the wear and tear of indoor life.

The primary ingredients of a fertilizer are listed as NPK, representing the percentage of nitrogen, phosphorus and potassium. Other elements may be present in varying amounts. Plants have differing needs for a particular element, consequently a range of specialized fertilizers is produced to suit these requirements. Some examples are the African violet and cymbidium orchid formulations.

The best approach is to find a couple of good, all-round fertilizers that foster strong, balanced growth. Any special food may be added as a supplement.

Feeding is useful to prolong the intervals between repotting, although no amount really compensates for a root system that is thoroughly pot-bound. Pot-bound plants are unable to grow enough feeding roots to absorb the food and much is wasted via the drainage water. Whenever a plant fails to respond as it has in previous seasons, a quick inspection of the root-ball indicates whether repotting should take place.

TYPES OF FERTILIZER

Animal manure
In the good old days the local milkman's horse courteously left behind the makings of liquid manure. Cow and sheep droppings are also suitable for preparation into manure tea and in the country were widely used. Animal manures vary in the amounts of plant nutrients they contain. Old manures are generally very poor sources of nitrogen, but fresh manures may contain too much. Some manures decompose too quickly to be suitable for potting mixtures, and some may contain weed seeds.

Modern fertilizer preparations give predictable results and are easy to apply. There are two main types — the liquid concentrates and the dry formulations. Both types provide the plant with the essential growth nutrients and give equally good results. The dry fertilizers are applied less frequently whereas the liquids are used regularly.

Liquid fertilizers
The best known of these are the fish and seaweed products which are diluted in tepid water and applied to the soil at the time of watering. If you find the smell a trifle offensive, there are deodorized brands available.

These products are most satisfactory for foliage and flowering types alike. Various other liquid concentrates are available and all are suitable as a beneficial supplement to the basic fertilizer incorporated into the growing medium. They must dissolve completely before applying them to the plant.

Dry fertilizers
Dry fertilizers are usually incorporated into the growing mix during preparation, or sprinkled onto the surface as a

top dressing throughout the plant's life. Probably the safest of these are the long-life prilled or pelleted formulations similar in shape to ball-bearings. The walls of the prills allow moisture to percolate both ways and take the nutrients into the surrounding soil at a controlled rate. A number of them have a specified life which indicates the expected duration of feeding achieved by the recommended dosage. In cool latitudes, the growing season is often short, so it is not advisable to have a substantial reservoir of unused fertilizer in the soil when growth has ceased. To overcome this difficulty, choose short-term formulations of say 3 to 6 months. These give excellent results over a wide range of house plants with a minimum of fuss.

Plant spikes and tablets are another method of supplying food. The dry crystalline powders are dissolved in water and treated in the same way as the liquid concentrates.

WHEN AND HOW MUCH

The months of active growing are usually from August until March, when plant demands and responses are at a peak. The frequency of feeding is very much a personal decision based on your assessment of the plant and its response to the surroundings. In the chapter on watering, the piggy-back plant and the snake plant were compared as high and low users of moisture. They use fertilizer in a similar way. Thus feeding must be tailored to each plant's needs, the time of the year and the position in the home.

Plants in rooms receiving poor natural light will never use high levels of fertilizer satisfactorily and indeed may suffer if overfed. Only those growing in well-lit positions should be given supplementary liquid feeding during the cooler times of the year.

The temptation to adopt the approach that if one drop is good, two are better, must be resisted. Plants can die from a single overdose.

Some points to remember when feeding plants are to:
- apply only to moist soil to prevent root burning;
- use only at the recommended rate. All fertilizers are concentrates and will burn if used incorrectly;
- feed only according to the need, and not on a rote basis that 'Today is Tuesday and therefore feeding day!';
- stir liquid and crystalline forms slowly into tepid

15

water and use only when completely mixed and dissolved;

- flush out the soil at least monthly with clean warm water to leach excess fertilizer and prevent a harmful build-up of salts;
- add enough liquid to each container to ensure the growing medium is thoroughly wetted and some drains from the holes;
- apply liquid feeds from the top of the pot only;
- withhold feeding during the cooler months in cold and/or low-light situations.

REPOTTING

REPOTTING IS a task often overlooked, yet it is important for house plant health.

While a plant grows visibly above the soil, the root system is exploiting the unoccupied areas in the medium for moisture and food. The growing or potting medium is not inexhaustible and must be supplemented with food and new mixture as the roots deplete the initial supply. The analogy to mining is appropriate — eventually the soil becomes exhausted. This is hastened by the abundant soil microflora which live in the organic matter. Thus the original properties of a potting mixture alter and its capacity to sustain growth diminishes.

FREQUENCY OF REPOTTING

It is neither possible nor wise to set hard and fast rules for frequency of repotting: the need will vary according to the situation. In general, repotting is necessary when:

- the frequency of watering increases;
- the drainage rate slows or increases noticeably;
- growth stagnates;
- root masses can be seen at drainage holes;
- plants have not been repotted for 2 years;
- the aesthetic balance between the plant and the pot size is lost.

A plant which requires water every 24 hours needs repotting. *Coleus*, for instance, has a vigorous root system which rapidly fills the pot. Sustained cramping of the roots checks growth and eventually lowers the quality of the plant. In this case a larger pot is needed to provide more mix for water storage.

Soil-based media, notably those incorporating clay and

a low percentage of organic matter, are prone to muddying. The structure breaks down, impeding drainage and reducing essential oxygen supplies to the roots. Conversely, a sandy mix can be expected to drain faster once the organic matter is used up. Neither condition is acceptable and repotting ought to be done promptly.

During the growing cycle, the spring flush is most vigorous, summer growth continues at a sustained level, and in autumn a slow-down occurs. Should a plant suddenly stagnate when it grew well previously, it probably needs repotting. A quick inspection of the root-ball highlights the problem — usually a solid tangled mass lacking space for new root development.

The pot-bound (or root-bound) plant suffers food and water stress. In extreme instances a plug of roots blocks the drainage holes and forms a mat in the saucer. It is impossible to repot such cases without a severe check to the plant and for this reason alone, regular repotting pays dividends.

The philodendron family is an interesting group. They have 'roving' root systems which quickly locate the nearest drainage hole leaving the bulk of the growing compost unused. Such roots are best coaxed back into the pot or cleanly cut away.

The aesthetic balance between pot and plant deserves attention as plants develop. Repotting is a way of correcting imbalance and supplying fresh compost.

PROCEDURE

Repotting can be undertaken all year round, though preferably from late winter to mid-summer. Local climatic conditions affect these times and some adjustment is advisable. A plant which urgently needs repotting should be done at any time including winter, except when a major disturbance to the roots is essential and the conditions indoors are cold.

Always have on hand a good supply of the following:
- clean pots of various sizes
- moist potting mixture
- stakes, labels, ties
- clean, sharp secateurs
- crocks if required.

Pots are measured across the top, although two 12 cm containers may well differ in volume. Normally plants

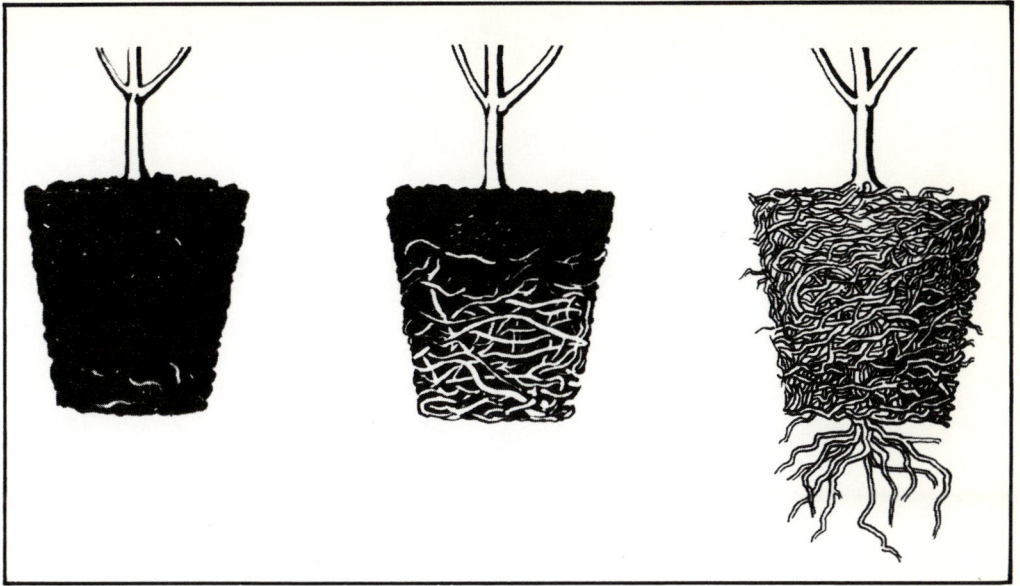

Repotting The plant at the left has plenty of unused compost. **Centre** *This plant is ready for potting on.* **Right** *This plant is completely pot-bound.*

progress one to two pot sizes, for example from a 10 cm to a 12 cm or 15 cm size. Never use an oversized pot simply because the correct one is unavailable, or to save repotting later on. The tendency is for the unused soil to be cold and sour with the result that the plant deteriorates. It is far better to repot a number of times in a season than to go for a 'once and for all' solution. The potting mix must be thoroughly moist. Sharp secateurs are used to prune leggy growth and remove damaged or dead roots. Blunt implements will bruise the tissue and retard fast healing.

Before the plastic pot became commonplace, most containers had only one drainage hole at the base. This tended to become blocked by the potting compost unless broken pots or stones (crocks) were placed over it. For this type of container, 'crocking' is still recommended, but just sufficient to prevent the mix blocking the hole. Ten centimetres of crocks will do no better a job than one or two pieces. With the modern plastic pot offering superior drainage, and with the improved potting mixes, 'crocking' is unnecessary.

The aim of repotting is to move the plant into a new container with the least possible disturbance. The root-ball of the plant must be completely moist but not soggy wet. Sloppy soil may fall away and break off valuable roots. If too dry, the soil and many of the roots will adhere to the old pot.

19

The palm is well overdue for repotting. Set the plant in the new pot so that the base of the trunk is just covered. Cover the roots entirely.

Evenly moist soil should slide out of the pot cleanly and easily with little damage to the root system. Support the plant by placing the stem or shoots between your fingers at soil level. Invert the pot and tap the rim sharply on a solid surface. Carefully lift away the pot and gently remove the upper crust of old soil and some from the base. Root pruning is sometimes needed. Be careful — the harder the pruning, the greater the shock to the plant and the longer it takes to recover. Spent mix and plant matter must never be mixed in with the fresh medium. Add sufficient mix to the new container to almost bring the root-ball to the level desired. Centre the plant and add more soil until all the space is filled, and the old soil–ball is just covered.

Make sure you leave enough space for water between the top of the soil and the top of the pot. Pots overfilled with soil are difficult to water accurately. Firm the plant and the new soil gently, and water thoroughly.

Stakes and other supports should be positioned during potting and not afterwards, as they may damage the roots.

Lush growing plants should not be repotted until the growth becomes less soft and sappy. Soft growth damages readily and may suffer a set-back unless care is taken. If you cannot avoid repotting, enclose the entire plant in a clear plastic bag with some breathing holes to lessen the shock. Re-establishment in the household environment is assured by gradually giving the plant more air over a few weeks.

THE POTTING MIX

The history of potting mixes shows that plants grow in all manner of materials provided they supply the essential elements for a healthy root environment.

The best indicators that a potting mix is suitable are vigorous, healthy top growth and a root system to match. To succeed the potting mix must provide:

- support (stability)
- adequate moisture
- oxygen to the roots
- food

and remain physically stable.

There are many different mixes available for both specialist and general use. Some are 'lighter' in mass and are unable to balance the top growth of tall plants. A mix which allows too much sideways movement of the stems is undesirable because this hinders root establishment. Heavier, soil-based mixes are preferable for these larger varieties.

The tiny root hairs are the primary providers of moisture. They in turn need moisture to function properly, but cannot thrive in a saturated, oxygen-starved environment. Thus a balance between the soil moisture retained and that lost by drainage ensures healthy roots.

Food for the pot plant is supplied via a base dressing to the potting mix, and by supplementary feedings. The long-life or slow-release fertilizers have a guaranteed nutrient content and release the nutrients over a set period, for example 6 to 9 months. Animal manures on the other hand have a variable nutrient content and are exhausted quite quickly.

The life of a potting mix is determined largely by the

type of organic matter used. Many traditional potting mix recipes recommended composted English oak leaves because of their nutrient content and their performance in the pot. They retain their form and do not break down rapidly. Garden compost is such a variable commodity that predictable and reproducible results are impossible. The quality relies upon the raw materials used and the system of composting. Compost often contains worms and ungerminated weed seeds and cannot be recommended for inclusion in potting mixtures. Unfortunately worms are a nuisance in potting mixes because they alter the drainage characteristics of a mix to the detriment of the plant.

Peatmoss and pinebark are excellent sources of essential organic matter and can be used in potting mixes. Decomposition occurs slowly and hence they remain stable longer. Other, less often used, materials are rice hulls, peanut shells, sawdust, bagasse and fly ash. The ability of all organic components to absorb water is important, not least during the cool months when infrequent waterings may cause the mix to shrink. Sawdust is especially difficult and it may be necessary to soak plants growing in it to ensure a thorough wetting.

Besides organic matter, potting mixes contain an inorganic component. Coarse sand and scoria are commonly used to open up a mix for better drainage and aeration. The sand and scoria being heavier are of particular value in mixes where large specimens are grown in small containers. Lightweight materials, such as polystyrene and perlite are also used. Peperomias, pileas, begonias and gesneriads prefer well-aerated mixtures and benefit from these lightweight materials. Polystyrene has the bonus of absorbing and retaining warmth in the root zone.

Soil is of course the basis of many potting mixes. The famous John Innes mixes were based upon loam in combination with peatmoss and sand. Soils, however, vary considerably and may not be suitable. For example, used alone the clay loams are unsuitable for those house plants with fine roots, and require major modification. Before soil is used it must be treated to remove pathogenic fungi, weed seeds and other undesirable soil life. For the home grower the soil-less media are better because the variables associated with soil are eliminated and the performance of each batch is predictable.

Vermiculite, a form of mica, is favoured by American

growers, often in combination with peat and perlite. Each is capable of supporting growth either alone or as a component and has peculiarities which must be understood.

The following are the base rules for making your potting mixes:

- Store all raw and finished products in clean containers.
- Mix on a clean surface and use clean tools.
- Label fertilizers clearly with their name and rate of application.
- Do not store mixes with added fertilizer for long periods.

When preparing the mix:

- collect and layer the moist ingredients in a conical pile;
- turn the pile top to bottom twice;
- add premixed fertilizers and turn twice more;
- add moisture if needed and mix again.

If a concrete mixer is accessible, use it.

The pH (measurement of the acidity or alkalinity) should be between 6 to 6.5 (slightly acid). Remember the pH scale is 0 to 14: with pH 7 neutral, 0 to 7 acid, and 7 to 14 alkaline. Each number represents a factor of 10 times ($\times$ 10). Thus:

- pH 6 is 10 times more acid than pH 7;
- pH 5 is 100 times more acid than pH 7;
- pH 9 is 100 times more alkaline than pH 7.

GENERAL UPKEEP

———

GOOD GROOMING is an important part of house plant culture. A well-grown but poorly maintained plant loses much of its beauty if dead leaves are left among the healthy foliage. Some judicious pruning here, a new stake there and regular cleaning enhance the impact of the plant.

Regular grooming should not be considered as a chore. The improvement in the plant's appearance makes it well worth the effort. Make maintenance a regular task and you will find that surprisingly little time is needed.

Maintenance tasks include:
- regular cleaning of the foliage;
- staking, tying and training;
- pinching back and pruning;
- removal of spent flowers and foliage.

CLEANING THE FOLIAGE

No plant looks its best if the foliage is caked with dust, nor can it function fully. The leaf surfaces are used by the plant to manufacture food and to breathe, in addition to the decorative value they provide.

An integral part of plant growth is light and this, in combination with adequate supplies of carbon dioxide, enables the plant to photosynthesize its own food. Dusty leaves are unable to utilize the available light to best advantage and cannot absorb enough carbon dioxide to maximize growth.

Cleaning includes both the top and bottom surfaces. A soft, dry cloth gently wiped over the foliage will remove most of the dust. The foliage must be properly supported on the palm of your hand to prevent any damage or snapping of the leaves. A light shower with tepid (slightly warm) water greatly assists in removing dust. When using a moist cloth be sure to rinse it regularly and wipe each leaf more than once to prevent grimy smears.

You may prefer the glossy appearance achieved by adding a small quantity of white oil to the water (at a quarter normal strength) or by spraying on one of the many leaf-shine products available in pressure packs.

Remember that hairy-leaved plants such as *Begonia rex* or the African violet family and ferns do not tolerate leaf-glossing materials at any strength. These plants are best dusted carefully with a soft brush or given a light shower with tepid water. Aerosol use is confined to the thicker, glossy-leaved varieties which include *Monstera*, *Philodendron*, *Ficus*, *Codiaeum* (croton), *Aspidistra* and ivy. It is easy to be seduced by the instant effectiveness of these pressure packs, but the temptation to spray just a squirt or two more may cause damage. They are handy and useful products if used strictly as directed. If you have some doubts, spray the leaf-gloss onto a soft cloth and gently wipe the leaves.

All plants have a special shine or healthy glow of their own which is encouraged by congenial surroundings and good cultural practices. Given these conditions, most plants will only need a monthly shower or wipe over.

STAKING, TYING AND TRAINING

When training a plant, remember that the growing tip is soft and easily damaged. As it matures, however, it goes through an elastic stage when it is possible to train growth readily. A little later, when the growth has fully ripened, this elasticity is lost, with the result that training is harder and the likelihood of leaves and stems breaking is greater. The best approach is to train and tie growth progressively, always taking care that the plant is allowed a little free play. Ties should be flat and broad, or round to prevent cutting into the tissue. Those materials which stretch are preferable because they permit the stems to increase in size without strangling them. The flat, plastic-coated tie-wire is not recommended because it does not stretch and constricts a rapidly growing stem unless it is adjusted regularly. No matter which tying material is used, it must be checked throughout the year and loosened or removed as necessary.

The climbing members of the aroid family — *Philodendron*, *Monstera*, *Syngonium* and *Epipremnum* — benefit from tying against a totem pole. The close contact between the aerial roots and the support encourages their rapid adhesion with the bonus of stronger leaves and stems. The vine-like species of the grape ivy clan, such as *Cissus antarctica*, *C. rhombifolia* and *C. striata*, are to some degree self clinging. Nonetheless they require training and tying if they are to be kept within manageable bounds.

For some varieties staking and tying is only a temporary measure until the young growth develops sufficient strength of its own. Plants falling into this category are frequently grown as single or multistemmed specimens, such as the rubber plant group (*Ficus*), the tree aralia (*Fatshedera*) and the tree begonias. The types and qualities of stakes vary depending upon the raw materials at hand. They range from sturdy tree fern poles to thin bamboo stakes suitable only for lightweight plants. Those plants which utilize stakes for permanent support require sturdy long-lasting ones, while the cymbidium orchid only requires a stake sufficient to support the flower stem for a few months. Wherever possible, stake the plant during potting up or repotting. Although things may look a little out of proportion at first, a slightly larger stake which allows for future growth can save a lot of extra work. The trick is to try to match aesthetic and practical considerations, not the least being the dimensions of the stake compared to the form of the plant, and the colour of the tie material.

Apart from those varieties mentioned earlier which need permanent support, staking should be viewed as a temporary adjunct. Soft sappy growth is frequently the result of overfeeding and poor light — if these are altered, staking is often unnecessary.

PINCHING BACK AND PRUNING

Plants differ in their response to cutting back or tip pruning. Generally regrowth is fastest when only the youngest few centimetres (the tip growth) are removed. Because some plants die if severe pruning is carried out, a progressive approach is advisable. Always retain some healthy leaves and only prune back to bare stems if absolutely necessary. Unfortunately not all varieties retain the ability to shoot from the old growth, so that the value of pruning and shaping as the plant grows is reinforced.

The warmer months of spring and summer are ideal for major pruning because they coincide with the periods of greatest plant activity.

Pinching back involves removing the soft growing point of a shoot. It is sometimes called tip pruning. It is carried out to thicken up the more vigorous climbers and trailers, as well as to promote new basal shoots. The multiflora begonias, ivies, impatiens and trailing peperomias benefit from this treatment.

Pruning yields an assortment of potential cuttings which must be culled so that only the strongest and healthiest are used for propagation.

REMOVING SPENT FLOWERS AND FOLIAGE

Not only do dead leaves and spent flowers look unsightly, but they are a potential food source for some plant fungi. It is a wise precaution to remove all spent flowers and leaves. Where they have fallen or died prematurely because of grey mould (*Botrytis*) or powdery mildew fungi, prompt removal assists in arresting the spread of the disease. Terrarium plants need regular inspection especially where flowering types are included. Remember that many fungi are opportunists eagerly awaiting the right conditions. By adopting good management techniques, the possibility of any attack on plant health is lessened significantly.

PESTS AND DISEASES

HOUSE PLANTS are no less susceptible to insect and fungal attack than plants in the garden. Nonetheless a clean plant brought indoors should remain so unless it becomes contaminated by unclean stock.

Insects and fungi do not spontaneously generate — the insect pest or its eggs are already present, as are fungal spores or areas of residual infection. These hatch or germinate when the conditions are right, often spreading to epidemic levels before damage is noticed. The indoor climate suits the pest which adapts its activity to the plant's growth rate. Winter time normally means a decline in most insect activity as growth slows, while spring and summer see a rapid build-up of pests and diseases, notably mites, aphids and powdery mildew.

The first measure to minimize pests and diseases is to buy clean plants. This is not always a straightforward task because of the difficulty in achieving and maintaining cleanliness in nurseries where the mix of species creates problems of control. Occasionally too, a pest escapes detection and is not apparent until some weeks later. Any new purchase should be isolated for a few weeks and checked regularly.

The second part of the strategy is regular inspection of plants. Outbreaks are best discovered early and effectively treated before they establish themselves.

IDENTIFYING THE PROBLEM

Ill health in plants is not always the results of pests and diseases. Yellowing and drooping leaves will result from water stress, draughts, excessive light and heat, starvation or natural old age. It pays to investigate the cultural conditions thoroughly and, if these are satisfactory, insect and fungal pests are two probable causes of ill health.

Positive identification of the pest or disease is important to ensure that the correct control is used. A pest and disease identification and control chart is included at the end of this section. If you are unsure of the pest, contact your local nursery or advisory service for assistance. Bear in mind though that the nursery staff will be less than pleased if you wave unhealthy specimens around their premises. Secure the sample in a plastic bag and remove it only when requested.

Control

The various methods of control are listed in the pest and disease chart at the end of this section. Should you decide to apply pesticides of any sort, it must be done thoughtfully and carefully. Many are toxic if used carelessly. The low toxicity types such as clensel and pyrethrum are preferable, however stronger and specific (to the pest) formulations have their place to clean up bad infestations. Be certain that the appropriate spray is used for each pest, e.g. a miticide for mite control. Damage to the plant may occur and the pest remain uncontrolled if the wrong spray is selected. The same approach is adopted when selecting and using fungicides.

Not all control measures for pests and diseases require the use of chemicals. In the chart on insects, for example, squashing aphids between the finger and thumb is a suggested control. Grubs and slugs are treated similarly. Some fungal diseases are eliminated or lessened by improving the cultural methods. A small fan to circulate the air effectively controls botrytis.

Whenever possible a balance between chemical and non-chemical means of pest and disease control should be sought.

If using pesticides, the following precautions should be taken:
- Store all sprays and equipment in a locked cupboard and ensure the labels on each container stay legible and intact.
- Follow the directions exactly and do not 'add one for good luck'.
- Do not mix sprays together unless the directions indicate it is safe.

- Spray during the cool of the day and onto dry foliage.

Aerosol sprays are widely available and are convenient when only one or two plants need treatment. They are particularly useful for flat dwellers and where the handling and mixing of chemicals is difficult.

As plant pests may become resistant to currently available pesticides in a relatively short time, no specific recommendations are made. Clensel and pyrethrum still appear to be effective. Recent progress in biological con-

INSECT	IDENTIFICATION	SYMPTOMS
Aphids	Small, leaf-sucking insect often in colonies on new growth and undersides of leaves. Pest colour varies through black, brown, red and green	Puckered and limp foliage. Stunted growth. Tell-tale honeydew — a sticky sweet secretion left by the pest. Often with black sooty mould which grows on the honeydew
Grubs and caterpillars	Mostly black, brown or green grubs often blending with foliage. Voracious appetite, will defoliate a plant if unchecked	Sudden holes in the leaf or chewed margins. Blackish droppings on the leaf or nearby surfaces
Mealy bug	White, fluffy insects, either singly or in groups along the veins, in the axils or undersides of leaves. Distinctive odour	Honeydew and stunting of new growth
Mites	Minute pests barely visible that feed in colonies on soft new growth and flowers. Heavy infestations are accompanied by a fine webbing over and between the leaves	Aborting, stunted, prematurely yellow and distorted new foliage. Multi-branched shoots. Misformed blooms. Transparent foliage
Scale	Small bubbles or blisters randomly scattered along stems and foliage. Almost transparent when young, darker, larger and stationary when mature. Brown, black or white	Heavy secretions of honeydew on foliage and nearby surfaces, accompanied by black sooty mould. Note: scale is sometimes confused with the sporing bodies of ferns which, unlike scale, are regular in distribution
Slugs and snails	Leaf-eating pests, especially of ferns. Soft, slimy creatures preferring moist surfaces. They hide in cool damp places, such as plant crowns, leaf axils and drainage holes of pots	Silvery, slimy trails on foliage and surfaces. Eaten leaves and flowers
Ants	Ants are often associated with scale insects and aphids. Ants will move the young pests around the plant and harvest the honeydew produced by them. Ants do not attack the plant but occasionally build nests in the dry soil. They	

trol — that is harnessing naturally occurring predators to control pests and diseases — offers exciting and environmentally better alternatives to a heavy dependence on chemicals. The biological spray Dipel mentioned in the chart is an example of a fungus controlling another plant pest, namely grubs.

The following chart lists the principal pests and diseases of house plants, their identification and suggested control.

SUSCEPTIBILITY	CONTROL
All, especially new growth	Squash between finger and thumb. Clensel or pyrethrum insecticides, or soapy water. Severe infestations require regular follow-up sprays. Systemic aphicides. Note: some aphicides burn ferns.
All	Dipel biological insecticide, particularly in greenhouses and ferneries. Finger and thumb. Specific insecticides, either contact, surface or systemic
All	Dab each pest with a cotton bud moistened with methylated spirits. Repeated doses of clensel or pyrethrum (these are contact insecticides only and must hit the pest to kill it). Systemic insecticides most effective
All	Increase humidity by misting above and below the leaves — beware however of encouraging mildew on susceptible varieties. Clensel. Specific miticides. Destroy all badly infested stock. Remove all flowers. Isolate affected plants until clean. Spray all adjacent plants. Note: some miticides burn ferns
All	White oil, specific insecticides. Note: white oil formulations will burn ferns and many hairy-leaved plants
All, especially new growth	Locate and squash the pest. Slug and snail baits on bench and soil surfaces. Liquid formulations are sprayed onto the plant and soil. Scatter pelletized baits sparingly and with caution
	disappear if the insect pest is eliminated. Ants are a handy indicator of an insect problem

31

DISEASE	IDENTIFICATION	SYMPTOMS
Botrytis	Fungus prevalent in still, humid conditions, especially if poorly lit	Browning of foliage, rotting of flowers. Fine hairs on affected parts
Crown rot, damping off	Fungi attacking plant stems above or below soil level. Seedlings are at high risk. Readily transferred from plant to plant if overcrowded or good hygiene is not observed. Prevents water movement throughout the plant	Total collapse. Soft leaf stems. Peeling bark or dead tissue on plant stems at ground level. Lack-lustre foliage. Seedlings with broken or kinked stems. Rapid leaf loss
Mildew	Fungus thriving in fluctuating temperatures. Attacks foliage and flowers	Whitish-grey patches or an all-over bloom on foliage and flowers. Distinctive musty smell
Root rot	Fungal pest preferring warm, wet growing conditions, especially poorly drained situations	Continual wilting with no response to extra water. Leaf yellowing and drop. Stagnant growth
Sooty mould	Fungus that lives on the sugary waste (honeydew) of aphids and other insect pests. Non-harmful but unsightly. Interferes with plant function to some degree. Does not disappear after the pest is killed	A black soot over any part of the plant usually in conjunction with live insects

Stem rotting fungus has attacked the bark, reducing water flow. Rapid leaf drop has resulted.

Mite has destroyed the growing tip and caused leaf damage to this Dizygotheca.

SUSCEPTIBILITY	CONTROL
All	Increase air movement. Avoid wetting the foliage late in the day. Improve light levels. Specific fungicides, especially the systemics
All	Improve hygiene and watering practices. Increase air circulation. Use treated mixes only for seed sowing. Discard badly affected stock. Specified fungicides, especially the systemics
Hairy-leaved types e.g. *Cissus*, *Tolmeia* and the gesneriads	Better air movement. Keep the leaves and flowers dry. Specified fungicides, especially the systemics
All	None. Discard all affected stock and potting mix. Sterilize the pots before reuse
All	Eliminate the insect pest and the mould will die from a lack of food — the sugary honeydew. Wipe away with a moist soft cloth

Mite is a common pest of many house plants. The young leaves of Fatshedera show the typical wrinkling caused by the pest.

Scale forms large dark blisters on the fern frond. They are easily distinguished from the smaller regularly placed spore vessels.

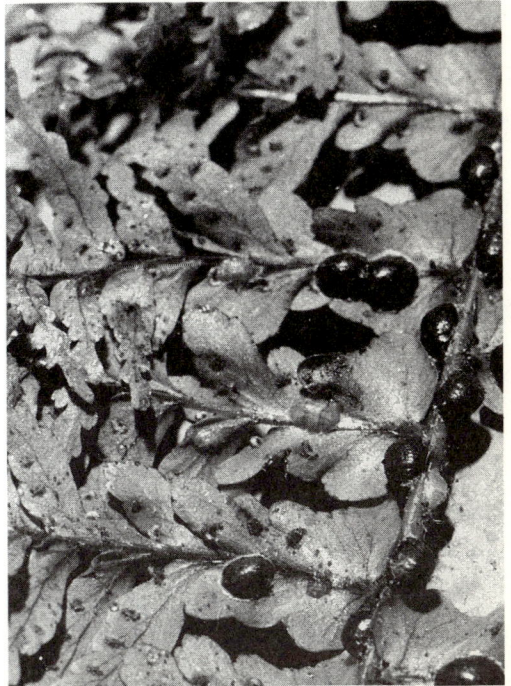

GUIDE TO THE AILING PLANT

When plants are stressed or unhappy with the surroundings, they exhibit certain symptoms. Generally it is the foliage that shows up a problem even though the cause may be at root level. Sometimes it is a reaction to less than favourable conditions such as a draught.

Remedial action involves consideration of the whole plant, starting with the root system to ascertain its soundness and, progressing upwards, assessing general health. Not all ill-health in plants is the result of pest or disease attack. Thus, a careful appraisal of the growing environment is required.

SYMPTOMS	CAUSE	REMEDY
Bud and flower drop	Poor light and stuffiness	Try to increase light and air circulation. Check the cultural notes for heat tolerance
	Reaction to being moved	Flower-drop is sometimes a temporary reaction to a new situation
	Insect or disease attack	Eliminate any pest or disease
Colour loss	Poor light	Coloured-leaved and flowering house plants require good light to maintain colour. Move to brighter position
	Insect attack	Eliminate the pest
Leaf browning, black areas	Sunburn	Remove from direct sunlight
	Pesticide damage	Check spray strengths and suitability
	Leaf polishing material damage	Be cautious in using leaf shines
	Heat stress — humidity low	Relocate to airier position and mist regularly
	Insect or disease attack	Eliminate the pest or disease
Leaf drop	Too much or too little water	Aim for evenness in moisture of potting mixture
	Draughts — hot or cold	Seal up cracks or move the plant
	Natural old age	The loss of the odd leaf is acceptable.
	Reaction to being moved	Rapid loss indicates bad culture
	Insect or disease attack	Eliminate the pest or disease
Leaf yellowing	Water stress	Adjust the watering
	Excessive light	Reduce light levels
	Lack of food	Starved plants are often pale green and lack vigour. Repot as needed, and feed
	Insect or disease attack	Eliminate the pest or disease
Spindly growth	Poor light, often with too much heat and food	Better light. Feed only when light levels are adequate
Stagnant growth	Poor light	Better light
	Inadequate food	If growth does not respond to feeding
	Pot-bound roots	inspect the roots. If healthy repot; if
	Unhealthy roots	unsound discard the plant. Note that some plants are dormant in winter
Wilting	Water stress	A healthy plant responds quickly when dry.
	Heat stress	A waterlogged plant cannot absorb water properly and stays wilted. Adjust the watering
	Air stuffiness and poor air movement	Improve air movement
	Insect attack	Eliminate the pest

GUIDE TO THE AILING PLANT

PROPAGATION

THE ART of plant propagation has stayed much the same over the centuries, with the biggest advances during the last 30 years or so. The simple cutting-in-a-hole approach has advanced and adopted new technology until today tissue culture or micropropagation is widely applied.

Propagation is used to reproduce the species while developing superior and specialized forms. The humble cyclamen, *C. persicum*, for example, has evolved into the multiplicity of forms and colours now available through selective breeding.

Seed is the commonest method of propagation, with cuttings, division and tissue culture being equally important.

PRINCIPLES OF PROPAGATION

Some essential points for successful propagation are to:
- use only clean stock;
- select only stock that is true-to-type;
- provide optimum conditions for rapid and healthy propagation;
- practise good hygiene.

Clean stock

Clearly, healthy plants cannot be produced from diseased material. Seed from reputable sources is generally very good, with any failure being due to factors other than seed contamination. The destructive damping-off fungi are air-, soil- or water-borne, so special care is necessary to prevent contamination of home-grown seed. This is assisted by isolating the seed vessel from the soil and by careful watering to avoid any splashing of fungal spores.

Similarly, cuttings are taken from high up on the plant. A quick rinse under running water is beneficial. If poor-quality stock is the only source of supply, subsequent propagations should aim to improve and strengthen the plant.

Trueness-to-type
Vegetative propagation, that is by use of plant material other than seed, permits precise replication of the parent plant. Seedling populations, on the other hand, are inherently diverse. This diversity is used for selecting new cultivars which are then perpetuated vegetatively. Similarly, 'sports' do occur on existing varieties, for example a pink-flowered shoot on a red azalea. These can be propagated by cuttings.

Variegated plants are unstable and may have shoots showing completely green or cream pieces. Cuttings taken from these plants must show the correct amount of variegation to maintain trueness-to-type.

The propagating environment
The freshly-prepared cutting no longer has the support of the stock plant and must produce its own roots to survive. To promote root development, the plant needs a suitable environment. Ideally this means a source of bottom heat to stimulate root initiation at the base of the cutting, and a cool or humid atmosphere around the leaves to lessen stress. The small, electrically-operated propagation boxes fulfil these requirements. Too much light is harmful. Young cuttings are placed in semi-shade at first and slowly given more light once the roots have formed and growth begins.

Hygiene
Good hygiene is essential to success. Not only must the cuttings be clean, but also the pots, labels and implements, the propagating mix, the propagating area and your hands.

Occasionally, short cuts work. But miss out one vital step and good luck usually departs.

Propagating mix
The important factors for propagating mixtures are that they drain well yet retain sufficient moisture, are warm and stimulate root growth.

The standard mix comprises three parts by volume of washed river sand to one part by volume of moist peat-moss. This is a tried and tested mixture which gives excellent results. It is best to begin with this mixture and experiment with other materials such as perlite, vermiculite and polystyrene once you are having success.

Dry peatmoss cannot be moistened properly once the cutting is in place, and must never be used in this way. Warm water is effective in wetting dry peat. A properly prepared mix will have the components and moisture evenly distributed.

Pot size

Correctly judging the balance between a cutting and the appropriate sized pot takes practice. Too large a pot means wasted mix, a loss of space and a mass of cold, wet mixture that retards quick root formation. A small 5 cm tube is appropriate for a small-sized cutting, say 5 cm long; although with the larger-leaved varieties, for example *Aphelandra*, a 7.5 cm tube is better.

The community pot is appropriate when there are many cuttings of the one variety. Do not place different types of plants together in the one pot as some develop roots and require potting-on before others. Constant disturbance of the cuttings retards root initiation.

STEM CUTTINGS

There are two types of stem cuttings: the tip cutting and the node cutting. A tip cutting retains the growing point, whereas the node cutting consists of sections of the stem and attached leaves. Node cuttings may be single or multileaved.

Preparation

Cuttings are generally 5 to 10 cm long, although this varies with each species and the distance between the nodes. A balance is struck between the leaves retained for plant function and those removed to reduce evaporation stress.

Once the length of the cutting is determined, use a sharp clean blade to make a smooth cut at a 45-degree angle. It is not necessary to cut exactly below a leaf. With node cuttings, leave only enough stem above the topmost leaves to protect the buds. Starting at the base,

Stem cuttings A piece of Aeschynanthus is cut into one tip cutting and three stem cuttings. Foliage is neatly removed from the base of the cutting. **Top** *The stem cuttings firmed into propagating mix.*

neatly trim off a third to a half of the foliage. All flowers, buds and diseased pieces are removed. All cutting material should be kept in a sealed plastic bag until final preparation.

Insert the section free of foliage into the potting mixture. Cuttings are either stuck directly into the mix (which must not be tightly packed), or into a hole made by a dibble. A dibble is a convenient length of wood or metal of pencil thickness kept solely to make holes in the propagating mix for the cuttings. It must be kept clean. Old knitting needles are ideal. The depth of hole made by the dibble should equal the length of stem trimmed free of foliage so that any air pockets at the base of the cutting are eliminated. Soft material cannot be stuck directly into the mix as it tends to break.

Firm every cutting carefully so that it doesn't wobble and to eliminate air pockets. Leave enough space between the mix and the pot lip for watering. Label each pot with the name of the cutting and date, and water at once. If your budget doesn't run to an electric propagator, clear plastic food bags are quite satisfactory. Place the pots inside the bags, but be sure the drainage holes are not covered. A few holes cut in the top will allow for air circulation.

Routine daily inspections indicate when water is needed, and help to spot and correct early outbreaks of pests and diseases. When roots appear, the young plant is weaned to less humidity and more light. Make haste slowly and the transition will go smoothly.

LEAF CUTTINGS

Some species are readily increased by using a leaf from the parent plant. The simplest leaf cutting is one where the entire leaf plus a section of leaf stem is used. African violets, peperomias and rex begonias are examples. The

Leaf cutting of the African violet with a cluster of young plants. Separate each and pot into tubes.

young adult leaves are chosen for best results — badly damaged, diseased or soft new growth is rejected.

Trim the leaf stem with a sharp blade to 3 to 5 cm, and carefully insert it into a hole in the propagating mix. Keep the leaf about 1.5 cm clear of the mix, firm gently, water in and treat similarly to a cutting. The young plantlets grow from the base of the leaf stem. The parent leaf is removed once the plantlets are established. Normally a cluster of plantlets grows from a leaf and each may be separated and potted up.

DIVISION

Plants commonly propagated by division have a suckering or clumping habit of growth. The fishbone ferns, marantas and snake plants are examples. Simple division entails splitting a clump into two or three and potting each portion. Old leaves and dead material are trimmed away.

Regular and thorough renovation ensures young vigorous stock and is the better method. The parent plant is

The golden snake plant does not remain true when propagated by leaf. The young plants lack the gold edge. Use division instead.

unpotted and the potting mix washed away. The entire
root and shoot system is clearly seen, and the best new
growths are chosen for potting up. The older, worn-out
pieces are discarded.

SEED

Seed propagation enables you to grow large quantities of
a plant quickly. Particular attention to hygiene and the
young seedlings is necessary. Clean seedpans are imperative for satisfactory results. Effective sterilization is
achieved by soaking all potting and propagating recep-
tacles in household bleach at 1 mL/L of water for 1 hour.
The seedling punnet or any shallow tray suits seed sowing. Adequate mix is contained to support germination,
and a short growing-on period. They warm up quickly
and are less prone to overwatering than deeper pots.

Commercially-prepared mixtures fit the bill if only
small quantities are needed. A 50/50 mix of peat and
perlite is satisfactory for most house plants.

Fill the seed tray to within 12 mm of the top with
moist medium, level and firm lightly. Water evenly and
thoroughly. Sow the seed as directed. Cover the top of
the tray with a sheet of glass or tautly stretched plastic
wrap and set in a warm position. A sheet of brown paper
is kept over the glass until the seedlings germinate. Gradually expose the seedlings to more light and air as they
grow, until they can survive in the indoor environment.

The young seedling is very susceptible to water stress
and fungal attack. A daily inspection is most important to
keep an eye on seedling health.

Once the seedlings reach a manageable size and have a
sturdy root system, they are potted into individual tubes
or trays for growing-on.

AIR LAYERING

Many house plants lose their bottom-most leaves as they
grow to leave areas of ugly stem. Others outgrow their
situation. Fortunately many respond to air layering, a
method of propagation that induces plants to grow roots
from their stems.

While the roots are forming, the plant continues growing unchecked. It is not until a well-developed root system is visible that the air layer is cut from the parent plant
and potted up separately.

Aeschynanthus
Spectacular foliage plants with unusual tubular flowers. They make good hanging baskets.

Aphelandra *The zebra plant combines attractive foliage with a colourful flower.*

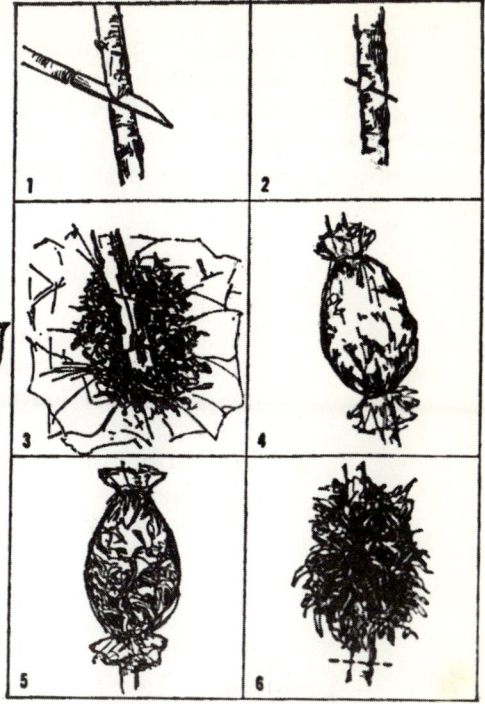

A pictorial representation of air laying. **1** *Notch stem with sharp knife or razor blade.* **2** *Insert piece of toothpick to hold cut open.* **3** *Surround with moist sphagnum moss.* **4** *Cover with polyethylene plastic; tie at top and bottom.* **5** *Roots can be seen as they start to form; be sure moss never dries out.* **6** *When root growth is vigorous, sever from old stem at dotted line. Repot in container of suitable size.*

Procedure

Assemble the following:

- thoroughly moistened sphagnum moss
- a clean, sharp knife or razor blade
- some clean plastic (clear) sheet
- some tying material
- a stake.

Using the blade make a shallow, upward cut 3 to 5 cm long in the stem. Take a handful of moist (not wet) sphagnum moss and work some into the cut. Use the remainder to surround the stem.

Enclose the moss with the plastic and tie securely at the top, the middle and the bottom. If the plant wobbles insert a stake and tie the plant to it.

The moss must be checked regularly and re-moistened if necessary.

The new roots will be visible through the plastic. Once the new root system is established sever the layer from the parent. Remove the plastic and while disturbing the moss as little as possible, pot up the layer. Firm lightly and water thoroughly. Enclose the top of the plant in a plastic bag with some holes cut for ventilation. After one week, gradually acclimatize the plant to the environment by giving it more air. Once established, remove the plastic bag entirely.

BOTANICAL NAME	COMMON NAME	METHOD OF PROPAGATION			
		SEED OR SPORE	CUTTING OR AIR LAYER	DIVISION OR SUCKERS	LEAF CUTTING
Achimenes	Hot water plant	■	■	■	■
Acorus				■	
Adiantum capillus-veneris	Maidenhair fern	■		■	
Adiantum fragrans	Maidenhair fern	■			
Adiantum hispidulum	Rough maidenhair fern	■			
Aeschynanthus	Lipstick plant	■	■		
Aglaonema	Chinese lucky plant	■	■	■	
Anthurium scherzerianum	Flamingo flower	■			
Aphelandra squarrosa	Zebra plant		■		
Ardisia	Coral berry plant	■	■		
Asparagus	Asparagus fern	■			
Aspidistra	Cast iron plant			■	
Azalea			■		
Begonia 'Cleopatra'			■	■	■
Begonia elatior	Rieger begonia				■
Begonia rex	Rex begonia	■			■
Begonia tuberous		■	■		
Boronia		■	■		
Bougainvillea			■		
Bouvardia			■		
Brassaia actinophylla	Umbrella tree	■	■		
Bromeliads	Vase plants			■	
Browallia		■			
Cacti and succulents		■	■		■

BOTANICAL NAME	COMMON NAME	METHOD OF PROPAGATION			
		SEED OR SPORE	CUTTING OR AIR LAYER	DIVISION OR SUCKERS	LEAF CUTTING
Caladium		■		■	
Calceolaria		■			
Camellia			■		
Campanula isophylla	Italian bellflower	■	■		
Ceropegia woodii	Chain of hearts	■	■		
Chlorophytum	Spider plant		■		
Chrysanthemum			■		
Cissus	Grape ivy		■		
Clerodendrum	Bleeding heart vine		■		
Codiaeum	Croton		■		
Coleus		■	■		
Columnea		■	■		
Cordyline		■	■		
Crossandra			■		
Cyclamen persicum		■			
Cymbidium	Cymbidium orchid			■	
Daphne odora			■		
Dieffenbachia	Dumb cane		■		
Dizygotheca	Finger aralia	■	■		
Dracaena			■		
Epipremnum aureus	Devil's ivy		■		
Episcia	Flame violet		■		
Erica	Heath		■		
Euphorbia pulcherrima	Poinsettia		■		

BOTANICAL NAME	COMMON NAME	METHOD OF PROPAGATION			
		SEED OR SPORE	CUTTING OR AIR LAYER	DIVISION OR SUCKERS	LEAF CUTTING
Exacum affine		■			
Fatshedera	Tree aralia		■		
Fatsia	Aralia	■			
Ficus benjamina	Weeping fig		■		
Ficus pumila	Creeping fig		■		
Ficus radicans	Creeping fig		■		
Fittonia	Nerve plant		■		
Fuchsia			■		
Gardenia			■		
Geranium			■		
Gibasis	Tahitian bridal veil		■		
Gynura	Velvet plant		■		
Hedera	Ivy		■		
Helxine	Baby's tears		■		
Hoya	Wax flower	■	■		
Impatiens	Busy lizzie	■	■		
Ixora			■		
Kalanchoe		■	■		■
Lamium	Aluminium creeper		■		
Lilium	Lily	■			
Maranta	Prayer plant		■	■	
Monstera	Fruit salad plant	■	■		
Nephrolepis varieties		■		■	
Nephrolepis exaltata 'Bostoniensis'	Boston fern	■		■	

BOTANICAL NAME	COMMON NAME	METHOD OF PROPAGATION			
		SEED OR SPORE	CUTTING OR AIR LAYER	DIVISION OR SUCKERS	LEAF CUTTING
Oplismenus	Rainbow grass		■		
Palms		■	■	■	■
Arecastrum romanzoffianum	Cocos plumosa palm	■			
Chamaedorea spp	Dwarf parlour palms	■		■	
Chrysalidocarpus lutescens	Golden-cane palm	■		■	
Howea spp.	Kentia palm	■			
Microcoelum weddeliana	Baby cocos palm	■			
Phoenix roebelinii	Pigmy date palm	■			
Rhapis spp.	Lady palm	■		■	
Peperomia		■	■		■
Philodendron cordatum			■		
Pilea		■	■		
Plectranthus	Swedish ivy		■		
Plumeria	Frangipani		■		
Primula	Polyanthus	■		■	
	Primrose	■		■	
	P. malacoides	■			
	P. obconica	■			
Pteris	Brake fern	■			
Saintpaulia ionantha	African violet	■			■
Sansevieria	Snake plant	■		■	■
Saxifraga stolonifera	Strawberry begonia		■		
Schefflera arboricola	Dwarf umbrella tree	■	■		
Senecio cruentus	Cineraria	■			

BOTANICAL NAME	COMMON NAME	METHOD OF PROPAGATION			
		SEED OR SPORE	CUTTING OR AIR LAYER	DIVISION OR SUCKERS	LEAF CUTTING
Senecio rowleyanus	String of beads		■		
Sinningia pusilla	'Doll Baby'	■			■
Sinningia speciosa	Gloxinia	■			■
Spathiphyllum	Madonna lily	■		■	
Stenochlaena palustris	Qld climbing fern	■	■		
Stephanotis		■	■		
Streptocarpus	Cape primrose	■	■		■
Syngonium	Goosefoot		■		
Tolmeia	Piggy back plant				■
Tradescantia	Wandering Jew		■		

Part 2

FLOWERING AND FOLIAGE PLANT DESCRIPTIONS

THE PLANTS described in this section provide the main sources of colour for the home. Some species are described in detail, each with an easy-care guide: these plants will most surely succeed in cooler climates. They are listed in alphabetical order of botanical names. Following these detailed descriptions are brief descriptions of a selection of some other rewarding flowering plants. At the end of the section is a chart which indicates which flowering plants are permanent or temporary residents indoors, and in which season each is likely to flower.

An alphabetical code is included for each plant to indicate its main cultural requirements of light, temperature, watering and environment. These codes correspond with the house plant guide at the end of the book, and the flowering plant guide at the end of this section.

CODE KEY

LIGHT LEVELS

A low to medium light levels
B medium to bright filtered light

TEMPERATURE

C cool, minimum 7°C at night
D warm, minimum 15°C at night

WATER REQUIREMENTS

E water thoroughly, allow to dry (not completely) between waterings
F keep evenly moist

SUITABLE ENVIRONMENT

G unheated greenhouse
H permanent indoor growing
J only temporary indoor use
K fernery

SPECIAL FEATURE

P perfumed

HARDINESS RATING

*   easy to grow, very hardy
**   medium-to-easy to grow, hardy
*** difficult to grow, requires extra care

FLOWERING HOUSE PLANTS

Aeschynanthus Lipstick plant

Aeschynanthus The glossy foliage of the lipstick plant is always attractive.
The flowers add further interest.

B D E H ******

EASY CARE GUIDE

LIGHT Dull to well-lit, no direct sunlight. Some varieties, for example *A. obconicus*, resent bright light. Seek advice on each type.

TEMPERATURE 10° to 30°C, optimal 15° to 20°C. Frost tender.

WATERING Moist during growing season, drier in winter. Use of tepid water avoids the yellowish blotching of foliage.

FEEDING Spring to autumn. Avoid high nitrogen formulations. Do not feed during resting period.

REPOTTING Spring to early autumn. Avoid root damage. Use African violet potting mix, firm lightly and water in. Keep slightly pot-bound.

PESTS AND DISEASES Aphids, mealy bug and mite. Root rot.

PROPAGATION Seed and cuttings.
Seeds Very fine, often attached to a thin filament. Sow thinly on the surface of a sieved, moist medium. Do not cover. Maintain a temperature of 22 to 25°C. Prick off into clumps when large enough to handle.
Cuttings Spring to autumn. Take pieces of at least three to four pairs of leaves, cut off the bottom pair and insert the cutting into a three part sand to one part peat mixture. Firm and water well, place in a warm position with filtered light. Pot the young cuttings, say three to four per 10 cm pot, once new growth begins.

THE AFRICAN violet family, Gesneriaceae, contains many delightful and colourful plants suitable for indoor culture. But many gesneriads cause disappointment because of their specific requirements. The lipstick plant, *Aeschynanthus*, with its colourful flowers and variety of foliage is a hardier plant than most gesneriads.

The aeschynanthus is a superb hanging basket specimen, developing long trailers which respond to tip pruning. The thick leathery leaves endow the plant with a degree of hardiness against the drying effects of air-conditioning and heating.

They are delightful pot plants, although large plants may become top heavy. A newer variety, *A.* 'Fireworks', is naturally bushy and well-suited to pot culture.

The developing flower emerges from its tubular calyx in the fashion of a lipstick, providing the inspiration for its common name. The unusual flowers always excite comment. In some species the calyx is more spectacular than the flower, while in others it is an added attraction. Flowering occurs primarily in winter and spring, although *A. bracteatus* produces its pillar-box red lipsticks year-round.

Leaf shape and colour varies. Apart from the usual shades of green, there is a variegated form and two with brown and green marbling — *A. marmoratus* and *A.* 'Black Pagoda'. Flower colour is predominantly in the reddish tonings although *A. marmoratus* is greenish and *A.* 'Black Pagoda' scarlet, yellow and black.

In its native habitat, *Aeschynanthus* grows on other plants — it is an epiphyte. It does not feed on the plants but uses them only for support. When cultivated, it thrives in humus-rich potting mixtures which drain well yet retain sufficient moisture for growth.

Lipstick plants have a definite resting period during the winter, when watering is kept to a minimum. Wherever possible this should occur without the undue stress of heating, which causes shrivelling of the foliage and eventual leaf drop if the soil becomes too dry. Watering during this period should aim to keep the plant turgid without stimulating any new growth. Naturally plants in heated rooms demand more water than those in cool areas.

Anthurium scherzerianum

Anthurium scherzerianum Despite its exotic appearance, this flamingo flower gives months of colour with little fuss.

B D F H ******

EASY CARE GUIDE

LIGHT Well-lit, filtered light; no direct sun.
TEMPERATURE 12 to 30°C, optimum 15 to 24°C.
WATERING Moist when plants are actively growing. Drier in winter — in cool rooms this is essential to prevent root rot in cold wet soil.
HUMIDITY Keep moist sphagnum moss around the stem. Mist the foliage daily in warm dry atmospheres. Foliage must be dry by evening to prevent leaf blotch.
FEEDING Spring to autumn. Weak doses frequently to stimulate leaf production and enhance flower colour. Slow-release types used sparingly are excellent.
REPOTTING Spring to autumn. Large plants can be kept in small pots by removing some old mix and replacing it with fresh mix every spring.
GENERAL CARE Clean foliage regularly with a soft cloth or a light shower. Use leaf gloss with caution and keep it away from flowers, buds and new leaves.
PESTS AND DISEASES Aphids, scale, mite and mealy bug. Root and crown rot.

THERE ARE many species of *Anthurium*, some of which climb and look like philodendrons. Many have insignificant greenish flowers, while others produce reddish berries. Besides *A. scherzerianum*, *A. andreanum* is the best known species. It has heart-shaped leaves and bright flowers.

Anthurium scherzerianum, the flamingo flower, is an excellent pot plant. Its tough, leathery foliage copes with heating and air-conditioning. The olive green leaves, oval to long in shape, develop successively from a slow-growing crown. The unusual and spectacular flowers emerge from the base of each leaf as it matures.

Flamingo flowers are epiphytic, requiring mixtures

with properties similar to those for bromeliads and cymbidium orchids — well-aerated with plenty of organic matter such as fine pinebark or peatmoss. Young plants are annually repotted to keep them growing. Older specimens, which have settled into regular flowering, need only be repotted when thoroughly pot-bound, say, every 3 years. If this is not practical, feed regularly.

The aerial roots which grow from the crown of the plant help to anchor the plant and absorb moisture and dissolved nutrients. They seldom become a nuisance and are best redirected into the potting mix, or enclosed in moist sphagnum moss.

Flowering usually covers the spring to late summer period. Flower colour is mainly orange, red, pink and white, with attractive two-tones also available. If you have a young plant, it is best to remove the first few flowers which are invariably weak and small. You will be rewarded with strong blooms subsequently. Extra crowns develop as the plant matures and these too will flower. Under no circumstances try to separate these because damage to the plant is invariably long-lasting. Dead flowers are cut off 5 cm above the base of the leaf. Do not pull these away while they are still sappy or you may snap off the leaf or a piece of the crown.

Anthurium scherzerianum is remarkably adaptable to cool conditions, growing well at temperatures as low as 12°C. Dull aspects produce disappointing results, so select a well-lit position with filtered light.

Aphelandra squarrosa — Zebra plant

B D F H ★★★

EASY CARE GUIDE

LIGHT Medium to well-lit; avoid direct sunlight.
TEMPERATURE 12 to 30°C, flowering 16 to 18°C. At lower temperatures growth stagnates and some older leaves may die. Needs extra humidity at high temperatures.

APHELANDRA SQUARROSA, the zebra plant, is an eye-catching house plant with dark-green and ivory foliage, and spectacular heads of golden flowers. The varieties available, such as 'Dania', 'Brockfeld' and 'Rembrandt', have tough foliage and a compact habit of growth.

Aphelandras prefer well-lit positions without direct sunlight which quickly burns the leaves. Poor light produces weak and spindly growth with little chance of flower formation. Where light comes from one direction only, rotate the plant regularly to encourage even development.

Aphelandras are not the easiest to flower in southern

Aphelandra Good, bright filtered light and a warm aspect suit the zebra plant.

WATERING Moist at all times, but drier in winter. Underwatering causes aphelandras to burn, while overwatered plants drop their bottom foliage rapidly and droop continuously.

FEEDING Spring to early autumn. Feeding in excess promotes soft, sappy growth which is accelerated under low light.

REPOTTING Spring to early autumn, using well-drained, humus-rich potting mix. A plant that has lost some bottom foliage can be planted deeper in the new container, but do not over-pot merely to achieve this. If the plant is leggy, keep the top growth for cuttings and discard the rest.

GENERAL CARE Clean the leaves of dust, and mist the foliage regularly to keep up the humidity and to deter mite.

PESTS AND DISEASES Aphids, mealy bug, scale and mite. Root rot.

Australia, but with adequate light and temperatures (around 12 to 15°C) good results are possible. Once the blooms fade, they should be pruned back to a pair of healthy leaves lower down so that the plant is kept compact.

Regular watering throughout the hotter months promotes vigorous growth. In winter the soil should be kept moist, but never wet. Root rot favours these cold wet conditions and once established is incurable. In common with most tropical house plants, adequate humidity overcomes leaf-tip browning.

PROPAGATION Cuttings are taken in spring and autumn. Select a strong tip cutting with two to three pairs of leaves. Remove the bottom pair cleanly with a sharp knife, and dip the base into a hormone rooting powder. Insert the cutting into a propagating mix of three parts sand to one part peatmoss. Water and enclose the top in plastic. Place in a warm well-lit position. Ventilate regularly to remove excess condensation. Once the roots are visible, gradually wean the plant until it no longer relies on the humid atmosphere of the plastic bag. Pot one cutting per 10 cm pot.

Begonia elatior

Rieger begonia

BEGONIA ELATIOR is another of the glorious flowering pot plants bought in flower to decorate the home. It is closely related to the 'Lorraine' begonia.

The Rieger begonia is a small, fleshy stemmed variety similar in habit to the impressive tuberous begonia, but

B D F H   ******

EASY CARE GUIDE

LIGHT Well-lit; no direct sunlight.

TEMPERATURE 15 to 25°C, optimal 15 to 18°C. Some air movement at higher temperatures.

WATERING Evenly moist, drier in winter. Never wet.

FEEDING Regular weak doses while the plant is growing.

REPOTTING All year using a well-draining mixture with plenty of organic matter. Do not repot during flowering.

GENERAL CARE Remove all dead flowers promptly. Cut back the stems to new side shoots after flowering. Stake as required.

PESTS AND DISEASES Aphids.

PROPAGATION Leaf cuttings spring to early autumn. Select a strong healthy leaf and trim the leaf stem to 5 cm. Insert the stem to half its length into propagating mix, firm gently and water. Aim for a temperature of 20°C in a warm, shaded position. After the plantlets emerge, pot them together into a 10 cm or 12 cm pot. Once established, remove the parent leaf.

Begonia elatior 'Schwabenland' The strong, clear colours of these begonias and their vigorous growth make them a must for indoor colour.

with no dormant period. It is a bushy grower and produces masses of bloom throughout the year. The colours come in many clear shades of red, yellow, orange, pink and pure white.

The foliage is attractively shaped and sturdy. It is a wise precaution to stake the shoots as they grow. Flowering stems are top heavy and break without some support.

A well-lit room with no direct sunlight is suitable. The blooms are quite substantial but do not appreciate stuffiness. Good air movement is beneficial. Keep the soil moist, but not wet.

The plant is fed regularly with weak doses of a balanced food until blooming begins. After the flowers finish, the stems are cut back to the side shoots and gentle feeding is begun.

The fibrous root system does not require a large pot. Repotting may be done after flowering finishes and the plant has been trimmed. Make sure you support the stems firmly between your fingers to avoid accidental breakage.

Anthurium scherzerianum *The hardy free-flowering flamingo flower that tolerates coolish temperatures.*

Bromeliads *This Aechmea has tough foliage which withstands central heating. Keep centre of plant topped up with room temperature water.*

Begonia elatior 'Schwabenland' The bright long-lasting flowers of this elatior begonia add colour indoors throughout the year.

Bromeliads *The bromeliad family is noted for colourful foliage and flamboyant flowers. They are quite hardy.*

EASY CARE GUIDE

LIGHT Bright filtered light; no direct sun.

TEMPERATURE 7 to 30°C, optimal 15 to 20°C. Frost tender.

WATERING Keep the soil just moist. The vase is kept full of water but emptied in winter for plants growing outdoors.

HUMIDITY Bromeliads tolerate hot and stuffy atmospheres but prefer humidity. Mist the foliage.

FEEDING Regular weak doses of a balanced fertilizer.

REPOTTING A fast-draining mixture similar to that used for cymbidium orchids. Bromeliads have a small, fine root system and do not require large pots. Repot only when completely pot-bound.

PESTS AND DISEASES Seldom troubled by pests.

PROPAGATION The easiest method for the home gardener is by division or suckers.

Division Propagate by division in spring to early autumn.

Suckers Only well-grown suckers are removed, using a sharp knife. Pot into individual pots and water sparingly until established. Alternatively suckers may be rooted in moist sphagnum moss.

THE BROMELIADS are a diverse and fascinating group of tropical plants, well suited to indoor cultivation. The term bromeliad covers the many species of the family, such as *Aechmea, Billbergia, Cryptanthus, Neoregelia, Tillandsia* and *Vriesia*. In their natural environment they are epiphytic, and may be found growing on the forest floor.

Many varieties have spectacular flowers and plain leaves, others are grown for their beautifully-marked foliage. The choicest varieties combine these two features. In some species the flower is short-lived but the flower spike remains colourful for many months. *Aechmea fasciata* has blue flowers and a pink spike; *Tillandsia cyanea* is violet and pink; and *Vriesia carinata* and *V. splendens* are yellow and orange-red.

The leaves are usually arranged in a circular pattern to form a vase in the centre. This vase should be kept full of water and the soil should be kept just moist. It is advisable to empty out the vase of plants grown outdoors during the cooler months, particularly if frosts are frequent.

Bromeliads are tolerant of fluctuating temperatures and grow as well in centrally-heated or air-conditioned rooms as in cool greenhouses or a porch. Naturally you should choose those species best suited to your conditions. Most prefer good levels of filtered light. This develops good flower and leaf colour. Direct sun will burn or scorch the foliage.

Each plant flowers only once, after which suckers grow from the base. The parent plant slowly dies and it takes from 1 to 3 years for the suckers to bloom.

Cyclamen persicum and its hybrids

B C F G J K P SOME ✳

EASY CARE GUIDE

LIGHT Well-lit; morning sun only or filtered light all day. No direct sun indoors.

TEMPERATURE 7 to 20°C, 10 to 15°C. At cooler temperatures, flowering is slower but each bloom lasts longer. In heated spaces bring them indoors for one to two days *only* at a time.

WATERING Keep moist at all times, but never wet. Drier once the leaves die off.

HUMIDITY Essential in warm, dry positions. Sit pots on saucers of wet pebbles, but pots must not sit in water.

AIR Plenty of fresh air, but avoid draughts.

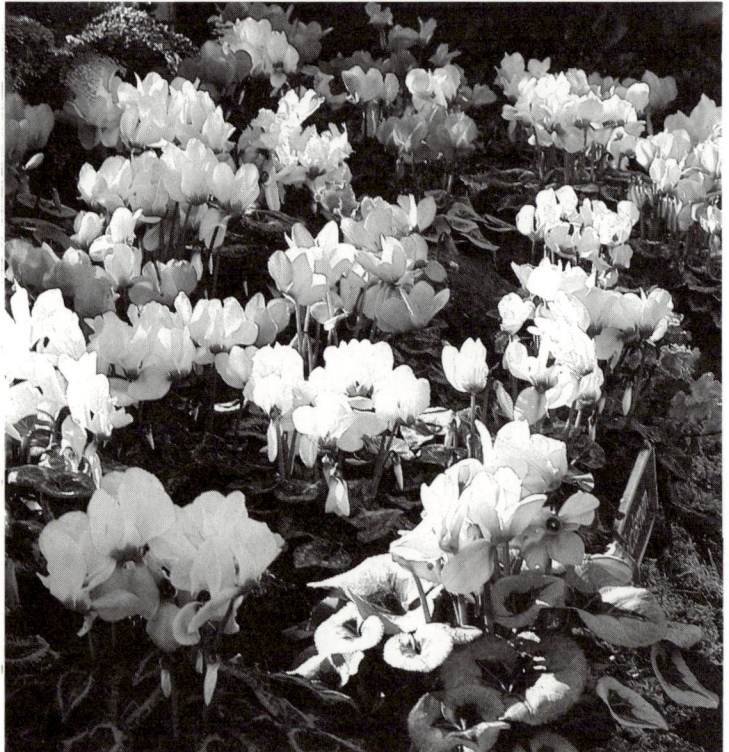

Cyclamen Few plants match cyclamen for months of bright colour. After flowering ceases, plant them in the garden. An ideal porch or bushhouse plant.

60

THE CYCLAMEN, or alpine violet, with its multitude of colours, flower and leaf shapes is one of the best and most generous flowering house plants. There is an extensive array of varieties to choose from, including the bold, large-leaved types; the intermediate growers of a more compact nature; and the delightful mini-cyclamen bearing a profusion of blooms above the foliage.

The mini-cyclamen represent a return to the original *C. persicum*. They have characteristically small foliage and masses of strong upright blooms and, occasionally, a distinctive perfume. The F1 varieties make vigorous compact growth and flower prolifically at an early age. Their colour range includes pastel shades of startling clarity.

The attractiveness of the cyclamen's leaves, with their unusual markings and shades, add interest when flowering ceases. Generally the leaf is deep green with a marbled whitish-cream overlay. The silver-leaf series provides a most appealing contrast between silver foliage and pink, red or mauvish flowers.

Each year new plants are released with flowers in white and in shades of red, pink and mauve. Some are pure colours and others are attractively striped or have a contrasting eye or edging to the petals. The petals may be plain, rounded, twisted, fringed or frilled.

Cyclamen are cold-climate plants. They deteriorate rapidly in central heating and air-conditioning, with the foliage turning yellow and the flower stems becoming weak and spindly. They thrive in a cool, well-lit, airy position such as an unheated sunroom, a porch or a fernery.

At no time must cyclamen dry out completely. They should be kept moist, but not wet. Fungal diseases such as crown rot and botrytis are avoided if you water directly onto the soil and avoid wetting the foliage. Overhead watering is deceptive because the water tends to run off the leaves without reaching the soil.

Selecting the right plant is important. Only plants with sturdy, lustrous foliage and plenty of buds and strong flowers should be chosen.

Once the flowering season is over, gradually withhold the water until the leaves yellow and wither. Do not attempt to remove the leaves until they are completely dry and snap off easily. During this drying period the soil must remain damp enough to prevent dehydration of the

FEEDING Regular applications of seaweed or fish fertilizer during flowering.

REPOTTING Cyclamen prefer plenty of organic matter, for example peatmoss, and excellent drainage. Young plants are potted on as soon as the roots fill the pot. Keep the crown of the corm (the point from which the leaves and flowers grow) well clear of the potting mix.

GENERAL CARE Remove spent flowers and foliage regularly. Do not allow these to die on the plant as the risk of crown rot is increased. Gently twist or roll the stems and pull away sharply.

PESTS AND DISEASES Aphids. Botrytis (grey mould), crown and root rot.

PROPAGATION By seed. Autumn sowing produces flowering plants some 12 to 18 months later. Use a well-drained seed-sowing compost, cover the seed very lightly and keep it in a dark spot until germination. Temperatures should be 13 to 16°C. Seed must not dry out during this critical stage. The seedlings are potted into tubes at the two to three leaf stage, and then progressively throughout the season.

corm. Each year failures occur because inadequate moisture is given during the hot Australian summer. As new growth appears, repot the corm using a well-drained, yet humus-rich, potting mix and place in a well-lit aspect outdoors. Maintain adequate moisture to promote steady growth. Plants may be grown from year to year, although the quantity and quality of the bloom usually diminish with age.

Euphorbia pulcherrima — Poinsettia

B D E H　　　******

EASY CARE GUIDE

LIGHT Well-lit to bright; no direct sunlight.

TEMPERATURE 14 to 30°C, optimal 16°C. Dormant plants may be kept at the cooler temperatures provided the soil is dry. Frost tender, thus strictly for indoor use.

WATERING Moisten thoroughly, allow to dry between applications.

FEEDING Regular weak doses before flowering commences. Do not feed during flowering or the dormant period.

REPOTTING Repot after flowering. The mix must have excellent drainage. Do not disturb the roots.

PESTS AND DISEASES Aphids. Stem and root rot, and petal blight (moisture on the bracts).

Euphorbia The long-lasting brightness of the poinsettia is hard to better. Poinsettias dislike draughts and wet feet.

THE MODERN poinsettia is an excellent flowering house plant that provides long-lasting colour. It may be purchased in flower, and given bright light will remain attractive for 3–4 months or longer.

The colourful part of the plant is actually a bract, the flower is insignificant and soon falls. The best known are the red poinsettias, with pink and white also available.

The foliage is a fresh green and contrasts well with the flowers.

The poinsettia must be kept in full light to maintain the colour and the foliage. Indirectly it benefits from the warmth and seldom survives for long at temperatures below 16°C. Sudden changes in temperature or draughts are to be avoided.

Poinsettias are extremely sensitive to wet feet and will not tolerate cold or sodden soil. Drainage must be first class, and water applied only when the soil is dry. If your plant turns yellow and the leaves drop off suddenly, overwatering is probably responsible. Once the plant is flowering, no extra feeding is required until the plant is repotted for the following season.

Many people discard the poinsettia when flowering ceases. You may wish to bring it on for a second year. After the bracts fall, let the plant dry out. Cut back the stems and keep the plant warm and dry; new shoots will develop. The plant is repotted into fresh soil, lightly fed and placed in a bright position. Keep the growth moving with weak doses of fertilizer until the new flowers form.

The sap causes a nasty rash and care is advisable.

PROPAGATION Not an easy task for the home gardener. Insert hardwood pieces without any leaves into propagating mix. Keep them warm and just moist. Pot up once roots are visible, but be very careful as they are quite brittle.

Impatiens   Busy lizzie or balsam

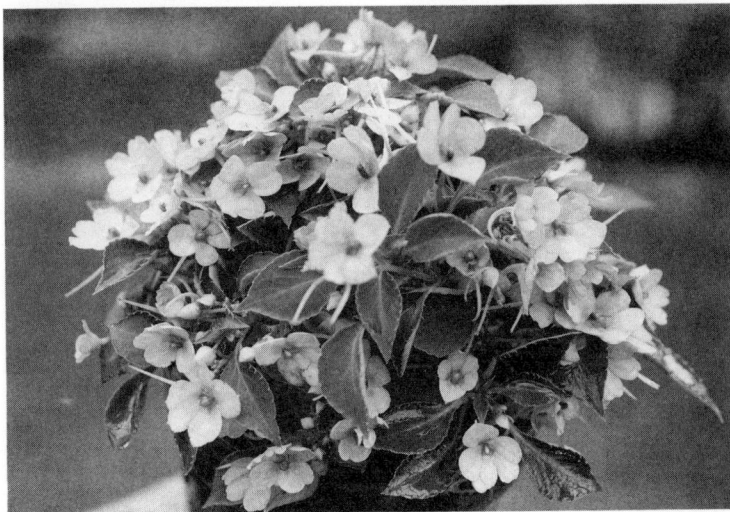

B D F G J K   *

EASY CARE GUIDE

LIGHT Medium to bright light. Morning sun only, filtered sun all day.
TEMPERATURE 12 to 30°C, optimal 15 to 25°C. Frost tender. *Note* Balsam is only suitable for growing in unheated greenhouses and ferneries during the warmer months.
WATERING Keep evenly moist in spring to autumn. Drier in winter.

Impatiens 'Pink Pixie' A gem amongst the busy lizzies. A compact grower covered in dozens of pink flowers.

FEEDING Regular feeding over the growing period, none during the winter. Choose those types recommended for flowering plants.

REPOTTING Spring to early autumn. A well-drained mix with plenty of organic matter is suitable. Pot on as soon as root-bound.

GENERAL CARE Regular pinching back of flowering shoots. Loss of flower early in the season is not important if the plant is sturdier and better shaped.

PESTS AND DISEASES Aphids and mite. Root and stem rot.

PROPAGATION By seeds or cuttings:

Seeds: Sow in spring to early autumn on a moist mixture, cover lightly. Place in warm, well-lit position and keep moist. Pot up once each plant is of manageable size.

Cuttings: Spring to autumn. Select a cutting 8 to 10 cm long without flowers. Remove the bottom leaves and insert into individual tubes of propagating medium. Keep moist and humid. Root formation is rapid, pot-on once established.

BUSY LIZZIE or balsam is a delightful and decorative flowering pot plant for adding temporary colour inside, or for long-lasting displays outdoors. The large range of varieties and the many colours makes it an essential part of any house plant collection. There are the low growing types, ideal for pot and hanging basket; the brilliantly coloured New Guinea hybrids with contrasting variegated foliage; and a deep-golden trailing species from Sri Lanka, *Impatiens repens*.

Balsam is a large user of water in the hot months and should not be left to wilt too often. The flowers will drop and the foliage turn yellow if the plant stays dry for too long. In winter, by contrast, balsam must be kept dryish. This assists it to cope with cold temperatures and keeps the root system healthy. The roots of overwatered plants rot, and the stems become mushy.

For best results, plenty of filtered light keeps the plant compact and flowering freely. The New Guinea hybrids need more light than other balsams. If your conditions are dull, choose one of the shade-tolerant varieties.

Impatiens repens 'Golden Dragon' This beautiful impatiens from Sri Lanka has golden flowers. A succulent trailer, it makes a spectacular hanging basket.

Temperature is important for successful culture. Balsam is frost tender, thriving best once the spring weather arrives. Some varieties cope with the cold better, others (including the New Guinea types) need more warmth. These are better kept in pots for ease of moving to warmer positions.

Balsam dislikes hot, airless conditions and thrives best if there is some fresh air during the heat of the day. A well-lit airy position suits best.

Feeding must keep it growing steadily but not softly. Weak growth is brittle and the plant flowers poorly.

The flowering stems need shortening back to new growth lower down throughout the growing season. They have a tendency to be lanky if left unpruned. It is best to carry out any major pruning in March to early April, or wait until October. Plants pruned during winter often rot.

Primula   Primula, primroses and polyanthus

B C F G J K P SOME **✱**

EASY CARE GUIDE

LIGHT Plenty of bright, filtered light.

TEMPERATURE 7 to 20°C, optimal 10 to 15°C. Move the perennial varieties to a cool, shaded position outdoors during the summer.

WATERING Keep evenly moist, not wet.

AIR Plenty of fresh air and good air circulation discourages petal rot.

FEEDING Regular weak doses of a balanced fertilizer.

REPOTTING Pot-on young seedlings regularly. Repot older plants in autumn. A general-purpose potting mix is suitable.

GENERAL CARE Clean away dead flowers and foliage.

Polyanthus provide an excellent source of winter colour for ferneries, patios and temporary use inside.

PESTS AND DISEASES
Aphids, slugs, snails and
grubs. Mildew and
botrytis.
PROPAGATION
Division: For polyanthus
in late summer or early
autumn.
Seed: All varieties
according to the
directions on the packet.

Primula obconica *A perennial form of primula with many heads of large bright coloured flowers. Keep them cool and moist.*

IN CONSIDERING colour for the home, there are many delightful annual varieties available. The primula family includes four excellent winter-flowering pot plants, *Primula malacoides, P. obconica* and the polyanthus and primroses. All are exceptionally hardy, easy to grow and bloom generously.

P. malacoides is the annual variety grown in the garden. It has soft, green foliage and masses of dainty flowers arranged in circles. Blooming starts from the base of the flower stalk to produce a delightful tiered effect. The colours are predominantly shades of pink, mauve and white.

P. obconica is the best known of the flowering primulas. It is a perennial variety and with care can be grown on for a number of years. The growth is sturdier than *P. malacoides*. The leaves are heavier in texture and have fine hairs which cause a nasty rash on sensitive skin. If you have sensitive skin, use gloves to handle the plant. Each flower is large and long-lasting. The main colours are white, blue, apricot and shades of mauve.

The polyanthus and primroses are popular garden plants suitable for temporary colour indoors. They are low-growing perennials with tough foliage and large two-toned flowers borne on short stems. Many are fragrant. There is a range of colours, many plants having a contrasting yellow eye or border to the petals.

Primulas thrive if given the same treatment as the cyclamen — a cool, airy aspect with plenty of bright, filtered light.

Artificial heating is detrimental and plants should not stay in heated rooms for more than 2 to 3 days at a time. Grow them in the fernery or porch and bring them inside for special occasions. Gentle feeding and regular watering is important. Yellow foliage is caused, most commonly, by drying out or starvation. The soil should be moist but not wet.

Saintpaulia ionantha African violet

THE MANY superb varieties of the African violet, *Saintpaulia ionantha*, are testament to its popularity for indoor decoration. It is an easy to hybridize plant, which has been transformed markedly throughout its cultural history. The once plain leaf and single flower is now available in variations of size, colour, shape and habit.

Flower colour almost encompasses the rainbow, with new releases every year. There are pure colours, two-tones, speckles and stripes. The original single bloom now comes in both doubles and semi-doubles; and the shapes include bell, star and tulip.

The trend some years ago favoured 'the biggest is the best'. Now a change in emphasis has produced a delightful collection of miniatures (minis), semi-minis and trailing varieties. These minis are perfect for the flat or unit dweller with limited space. The trailers are probably the most rewarding of all the violets, demanding less attention than the standard types and flowering freely in the right conditions.

African violets must have plenty of light before flowers are initiated, plus a regular supply of plant food. Direct or unfiltered sun burns and yellows the foliage and ages the blooms prematurely. Morning sun or day-long filtered light is ideal. Plants grown in the cooler southerly latitudes receiving poor light and heat may become semi-

B D E H   **★★**

EASY CARE GUIDE

LIGHT No direct sun. Morning sun or filtered light all day. Yellow or burnt foliage indicates excessive brightness.
TEMPERATURE 15 to 25°C, optimal 15 to 22°C. Frost tender, so remove plants from window sills during the cold months.
WATERING Evenly moist. Allow to dry out slightly between applications; drier in winter. Use only tepid or room-temperature water.
HUMIDITY Beneficial, but ensure leaves are dry before sundown.
FEEDING Regular doses of African violet food. Slow-release types give excellent results. Cease feeding in low light and low temperatures.

REPOTTING Spring to autumn. Keep crowns above the soil level. Select well-draining mixes with a high proportion of organic matter.

GENERAL CARE Remove all spent leaves and blooms by gently pulling the stems in a clockwise direction. Carefully rinse dust from the foliage using tepid water.

PESTS AND DISEASES Mite, mealy bug and aphids. Powdery mildew, botrytis, crown rot and root rot.

PROPAGATION By seeds or leaf cuttings.

Seeds Spring to autumn. Very fine seed needing a moist and fine mixture. Use a shallow tray and sow thinly on to the surface. Cover with plastic or glass to hasten germination. An unused fishtank with a fluorescent light provides the ideal environment. Space the seedlings as they develop, and put into tubes at the four to eight leaf stage.

Leaf cuttings Spring to autumn. Select the semi-mature leaves in the middle of the plant. Shorten the leaf stem to about 2.5 to 4 cm, with the cut at a 45° angle, and slit it lengthwise for 10 to 12 mm. Gently insert the stem into the propagating mix, for a half to two-thirds of its length, firm and water. Place in a warm position. Separate the young plantlets once they are big enough to handle and pot into tubes.

Saintpaulia African violets thrive under artificial lighting.

dormant. They will survive coolness (10°C) provided the soil is not sodden.

Regular feeding assists strong healthy growth and flowering. As each leaf axil produces bloom but once, new growth is necessary for continued blooming.

Overwatering is often the cause of most failures. The plant has evolved a fine, shallow root system for life in the humus–rich forests of central Africa. The leaf debris supplies nutrients, humidity, moisture storage and excellent drainage. A short period of dryness does not kill the plant but, if it is sustained, growth is eventually affected. Early morning watering is recommended to ensure that the plants are dry before sundown. In this way botrytis and other fungal pests such as powdery mildew are discouraged.

The decision is whether to water from above or below. Certainly watering from the base of the pot (that is sitting the pot in water and allowing it to soak upwards) eliminates leaf–blotching and ensures even wetting. But temporary oxygen starvation of the roots may occur and salt (fertilizer) accumulation in the upper soil is possible. Such salting is harmful and must be countered by regular flushing–out from overhead using warm water.

Overhead watering causes leaf–blotching if the leaf and water temperatures differ significantly, for example cold water on a hot leaf. Tepid water prevents blotching. Even so, plants with wet foliage should be kept away from bright sunlight until dry. If in doubt, water directly on to the surface of the growing medium.

African violets appreciate humidity. A daily misting with room-temperature water is beneficial (but not in direct sun) during summer and when heaters operate. Other growers prefer to sit the plants on a shallow tray of gravel which is kept wet.

Repotting is done throughout the year. Young plants in particular are potted–on as soon as the roots fill the containers. At each potting any of the youngest leaves that are losing vitality are discarded. Established plants which have settled comfortably into regular flowering may stay in the same size pot with an annual repotting being sufficient. The older leaves at the base of the plant are removed cleanly by gently pulling them in a clockwise direction. The spent growing mixture is shaken free, the plant is set deeper into a clean pot, and fresh medium is added.

The shallow or squat pot suits the African violet best, accommodating the natural habit of the root system. Plants grow and flower better if slightly pot-bound. Overpotting is inadvisable and can cause deterioration in root and plant health if the soil stays too wet.

On all occasions the lowest leaves and the growing crown must stay clear of the potting mix to reduce the possibility of crown rot. Crown rot is an incurable fungal disease which destroys the plant eventually. It is spread from plant to plant by contaminated soil, labels, implements, hands and gloves. Plants grown on capillary matting or watered from below in the same tray are equally at risk should one specimen succumb to the disease.

All infected stock is discarded immediately and a complete disinfection programme implemented using household bleach (1.5 per cent chlorine) at the rate of 1 mL per litre for a 60 minute soaking.

Sinningia speciosa Gloxinia

EASY CARE GUIDE

LIGHT Well lit; avoid direct sunlight. Excess brightness causes leaf yellowing.

TEMPERATURE Young plants around 20°C. Bud and bloom at 12 to 15°C.

WATERING Young plants kept moist, not wet. Mature specimens must never dry out — this causes bud rotting, flower drop and leaf yellowing. Water thoroughly and avoid wetting the foliage. Keep dry during dormancy.

HUMIDITY In hot weather sit the pot on a saucer of moist pebbles.

FEEDING Regularly during active growth and bud formation. Reduce the frequency as soon as flowering begins. Gloxinias are sensitive to fertilizer salts accumulating in the growing mixture and should be flushed once a month with warm water only.

PESTS AND DISEASES Aphids, mite and grubs. Powdery mildew.

PROPAGATION By seeds and leaf cuttings.
Seeds Late winter and spring at a temperature of 22°C. Sow the fine seed sparingly on to a fine pasteurized mixture. Keep evenly moist. Pot singly into tubes at the six to eight leaf stage.

Sinningia speciosa Gloxinias prefer filtered light, even moisture, and some protection from the heat.

GLOXINIA IS a tuberous member of the gesneriad family, that enjoys similar cultural conditions to the beautiful *Streptocarpus*. Gloxinias are hybrids of the genus *Sinningia*, specifically *S. speciosa*. Collectors of gesneriads whose conditions are not ideal for African violets find the gloxinia and other *Sinningia* species, such as *S. pusilla* 'Doll Baby', less demanding and quite rewarding.

Hybrids come in a variety of colours and combinations, including white, red, pink, mauve and purple. One of the outstanding varieties is the velvety, double red and white 'Gregor Mendel'. The newer varieties are more compact in habit and have smaller leaves less prone to accidental breakage.

Gloxinias thrive in plenty of bright indirect light. In summer conditions extra protection from temperatures above 25°C is necessary to prevent bloom stress. Bud blast or rot often occurs under these conditions, particularly if the air is dry and circulation is poor. Irregular watering worsens the problem. For this reason gloxinias thrive best in cool, airy rooms or glassed-in verandas with morning sun.

At the end of the flowering season slowly reduce the water and dry-off the foliage. Remove the tuber and store it in dry peat or sand at about 13°C. The tuber must not shrivel. In late winter repot the tuber into a potting mixture for African violets, ensuring the rounded part is set downwards. Keep it moist and warm, around 15 to 20°C, until the shoots emerge. As they grow, give the plant more light to promote bud development and a stocky, rounded specimen. Flowering normally begins 3 to 5 months later.

Leaf cuttings Summer. Cut a healthy leaf with about 3 to 5 cm of leaf stem. Insert the leaf stem into the propagating mix to just below the leaf. Firm carefully and water thoroughly. Enclose the top in a plastic bag with holes for ventilation and place in a warm, well-lit position. The young tuber forms at the base of the leaf.

Spathiphyllum — Madonna lily

THERE HAVE been many introductions to the range of flowering pot plants. Quite a few have fallen by the way-side, being too difficult for all but the keenest gardener. *Spathiphyllum* (the madonna lily), however, is an out-standing success, tolerating the wide range of conditions indoors.

Spathiphyllums are principally foliage plants with durable glossy leaves. As each growth matures an unusual hooded flower emerges. Generally these are a glistening pure white, gradually changing to green as they age. There are other less-decorative species with flowers of a greenish-yellow hue. Growth habits suit most situations, from the small and compact *S. wallisii*, to the arresting beauty of the larger *S.* 'Mauna Loa'. Most varieties are sweetly perfumed.

Although spathiphyllums come from equatorial South America, they adapt quickly to their new surroundings. However, direct exposure to either sunlight or heating causes foliage to lose condition and become tired. *Never* allow direct sunlight to strike the plant — it will burn and blacken in 5 minutes on a hot day. It is essential, if trans-porting the plant home from the nursery by car, that it is kept well away from the glass. Even in winter, foliage which is unaccustomed to bright sunlight will burn. *Never* leave plants in a closed car in the sun. Similarly, frosty mornings are a danger, as are hot or cold winds blowing through the windows.

B D F H P　　　　**✳**

EASY CARE GUIDE

LIGHT Dull to well-lit. No direct sunlight; suitable for artificial lighting. Plants in dark conditions may not bloom as frequently.

TEMPERATURE 15° to 30°C, optimum 15° to 22°C.

WATERING Moist, not wet; drier in winter, but avoid wilting. Use tepid water in winter to prevent root shock.

HUMIDITY Tolerates dry atmospheres, although leaf-tip burn may occur. Sit each pot on a saucer of pebbles which are kept wet. Mist the leaves daily during hot spells and when heating artificially.

FEEDING Spathiphyllums are both flowering and foliage plants, so they need balanced feeding. Feed while plants are growing or in bloom. Slow-release fertilizers are excellent.

REPOTTING Repotting each year is unnecessary. Plants have a small root system and do not mind being pot-bound. Choose a moist potting mix containing plenty of organic matter (not garden compost).

GENERAL CARE Regular grooming required. As each flower dies, *cut* the flower stem to just above the leaf and let it dry out completely before removing it. Any attempt to pull it out while it is green will probably break off a piece of the crown. Spent leaves are cut close to the crown and treated similarly.

PESTS AND DISEASES Aphids, scale and mite. Root rot.

PROPAGATION By seeds, suckers or division.

Seeds Seed ripens throughout the year. Sow at once onto fine moistened sphagnum or peatmoss; cover with plastic or glass. Bottom heat around 20° to 25°C ensures rapid and even germination. Wean seedlings as they develop before potting into individual tubes.

Divisions Spring and autumn. Not all varieties divide readily. Care must be taken to avoid damage to the crowns. Resist the temptation to cut into very small pieces as these may not survive. Use a sharp knife or secateurs to trim away all dead and damaged roots and leaves. Cut off all flowers before repotting.

Suckers Spring and autumn. *S. wallisii* in particular produces small suckers from the base. Remove the parent plant from its pot and carefully separate the best suckers. Pot these into small tubes. Replace the parent in its pot, adding extra soil. Place the divisions into a plastic bag until they have re-established.

Spathiphyllum *Fresh green foliage and sweetly scented white flowers.*

Streptocarpus   Cape primrose

B C F H   ★★

EASY CARE GUIDE

LIGHT No direct sun; plenty of bright filtered light. Artificial light is satisfactory.

STREPTOCARPUS belong to the gesneriad family which includes gloxinia, *Saintpaulia*, *Columnea* and *Aeschynanthus*. They are as diverse in habit as in flower colour. The most common are those forms which grow from a central crown, e.g. 'Weismoor', 'Constant Nymph' and 'Concorde' hybrids, but there are also a number of fleshy stemmed species that make very attractive basket and pot plants.

The bloom resembles foxgloves. There are pure coloured varieties and two-toned varieties with a splash of contrasting colour in the throat. Flowers come in shades of pink, blue, lavender and white, and are borne singly or in clusters on stout stems above the foliage. Flowers begin to appear in spring once adequate light levels are reached.

The flower stems which arise from the base of mature leaves must always be *cut* off.

Any attempt to pull them away damages the crown. Similarly the old leaves are cut off close to the crown and the leaf stump allowed to dry off before removing it.

Streptocarpus, like the African violet, thrives under artificial light and may bloom throughout the winter. However, while adequate light is required for strong growth, too much light causes yellowing and scorching of the foliage.

TEMPERATURE 7° to 30°C, optimal 15° to 20°C. To offset fatigue in hot weather, increase the humidity and reduce feeding to toughen the foliage.

WATERING Use tepid water; avoid splashing the leaves. Keep moist at all times, but drier in winter when plants enter a resting period.

HUMIDITY Good levels are important to prevent leaf-tip browning and general lack-lustre appearance. Sit plants on saucers of wet pebbles.

FEEDING Use fertilizers formulated for African violets. Avoid high nitrogen levels which promote sappy growth and few blooms. Never feed dry plants — water thoroughly first.

REPOTTING Early spring, using a humus-rich, well-drained mix. The leaves are brittle so care is needed. *Cut* off any old leaves close to the base. Ensure plants are set no deeper when repotting to avoid crown rot. Do not divide the crowns.

PESTS AND DISEASES Aphids, mite and mealy bug. Root and crown rot.

Streptocarpus *Carefully cut off the spent flowering stems close to the crown.*

PROPAGATION Seed, cuttings and leaf cuttings in spring and summer.
Seed Very fine. Sow thinly on a fine medium to allow development. Do not cover with soil and place in a temperature of 22°C. Keep moist at all times. When two to three leaves develop, gently separate and pot each seedling into a tube. Harden-off gradually.
Cuttings (fleshy-stemmed types) Select pieces 5 cm long, remove foliage from the bottom two-thirds, insert into cutting mix. Firm and water well.
Leaf cuttings Select a healthy leaf and cut crosswise into sections 2.5 cm wide; discard the top and bottom pieces. Insert the sections to half their depth into a propagating mixture of three parts perlite to one part peatmoss; firm and water. Cover with a plastic bag and place in a warmish well-lit position. Once young plants develop sufficiently, pot into tubes.

Although from tropical South Africa and Madagascar, the Cape primrose prefers cool night temperatures in summer. The flowers wilt and die quickly in hot and airless conditions.

The Streptocarpus are a fine, fibrous-rooted group preferring squat containers with more width than depth, and humus-rich growing mixes. Make sure that plants grown in hanging baskets drain readily as cold, wet soil causes crown and root rot. Plants suffering from wet feet generally remain limp, wilt rapidly in the warmth and are sluggish in growth. They do not respond to extra water. Treat your Cape primrose as you would the African violet. A little soil dryness is beneficial.

ABOVE Cyclamen persicum A generous flowering pot plant that gives months of superb winter colour. Keep cool, with filtered light and fresh air.

RIGHT Primula malacoides The well-known garden primula comes in a variety of pink and purple tonings, and white. They flower prolifically and are easy to grow.

BELOW Sinningia speciosa Attractive foliage and plenty of velvety flowers.

Saintpaulia *African violets The superb array of colours, leaf shapes and plant habit makes the Saintpaulia a must in every house plant collection.*

BRIEF DESCRIPTIONS

Achimenes
Hot water plant

B D F H   ******

Achimenes Easy to grow gesneriads for summer colour.

Small, summer-flowering trailers for pot or basket. Apply regular, weak doses of fertilizer until flowering. After flowering, gradually dry off the plant and store the rhizomes in dry sand. Restart in spring using indoor potting mix. Propagation is by seeds, cuttings, leaves or dividing the rhizomes.

Azalea

Glorious flowering shrubs for temporary indoor colour. Choose plants with more bud than open flower. A cool, well-lit and airy position is desirable. Mist the foliage daily in warm rooms and put the plant in the cool overnight. After flowering, move to a shaded spot outdoors. Propagation is by cuttings.

B C F J K PSOME   *****

Azalea 'Xmas Pink' *A beautiful plant for temporary winter colour.*

Begonia tuberous

B D F G J ✱✱✱

Begonia tuberous The tubers are started again in spring after a winter resting period. Keep the top of the tuber above the mixture and water carefully.

Begonia tuberous *The magnificent flowers of this begonia are best achieved in a cooler climate.*

Showy, large-flowered begonia blooming in autumn. The plant is started from the tuber in spring in moist peat and sand. Keep the hollow part of the tuber up and slightly above soil level. Pot into well-draining organic mix as they develop. Stake each growth. Gradually dry out after flowering. Store the tuber in dry peatmoss. Watch for aphids and mildew. Plants are propagated by seeds or cuttings.

Boronia megastigma   Brown boronia

The Australian brown boronia is famous for its attractive perfumed flowers in spring. It dislikes central-heating and prefers a cool, airy position. Mist daily and put the plant in the cool overnight. After flowering, move to a shaded position outdoors for 2 weeks before planting out. Propagation is from seeds and cuttings.

B C F J P   *

Boronia megastigma *The delicate perfume of the brown boronia is renowned.*

Bougainvillea

B D F G J   ******

Bougainvillea *Bougainvilleas make superb baskets, standards or clipped pot plants. The long lasting flowers give weeks of summer colour.*

Vigorous climbing shrubs with large clusters of vibrant flowers in summer. They make a superb basket, or trained as a standard specimen. Keep the potting mix moist while growth is active; drier in winter. Frost protection is essential. The double varieties flower freely. Colours include purple, white, yellow, orange and scarlet. Prune after flowering. Propagation is by cuttings.

Bouvardia

A small outdoor shrub with strongly-scented, pure-white flowers during summer and autumn. Fresh air is beneficial and, after 3 to 4 days indoors, rest them for a week outdoors. They are frost tender. Propagation is by cuttings.

B D F J P   *

Bouvardia *Pleasantly perfumed. Grow it in full sun and bring it indoors for a day at a time.*

Browallia

B D F G J   *

Browallia *These annuals are most effective for splashes of colour in ferneries, patios and indoors.*

The browallia is a small, free-flowering annual with attractive blue or white flowers during summer. It is frost tender. Propagation is by seeds.

Cacti and succulents

B C E G H J K   * **Cacti and succulents** *Excellent low-maintenance house plants for those with restricted space.*

The succulents, including cacti, range in size from the tiny stone plants to the giant column species. The crab and orchid cacti produce spectacular flowers while many other varieties are grown for both their flowers and attractive appearance. They are ideal house plants for the person with little time or space. They do not need frequent repotting, grow happily in small pots, require little maintenance and are almost pest free. Some are grown outdoors and used for temporary colour, others live inside permanently. Most are frost tender. Propagation is by seeds, cuttings or leaves.

Calceolaria

A brightly-coloured annual with purse-like blooms atop fresh green foliage. Colours are yellow, orange and red, with contrasting blotches or spots. Choose plants with plenty of bud. Feed the seedlings, cease once flowering begins. *Calceolaria* is grown from seed.

B C E G J **★★**

See colour plates.

Camellia

Camellias The camellia is a first-class pot plant. Bring them indoors for short periods while in flower.

B C F J K PSOME **★**

Camellias are notable for their beautiful flowers and lustrous deep-green foliage. In hot areas fernery culture is possible. Some varieties are suitable for hanging baskets. They are propagated by cuttings.

Campanula isophylla Italian bellflower

B C F G J K * The beautiful Italian bellflower, *C. isophylla*, is a hardy, summer-flowering basket plant. There are two varieties, 'Alba', glistening white, and 'Mayii', china blue. Feed throughout the growing period, cease after flowering. Prune off the old growth and keep drier over winter. Plant a number of cuttings per basket or pot. Propagation is by cuttings or seeds.

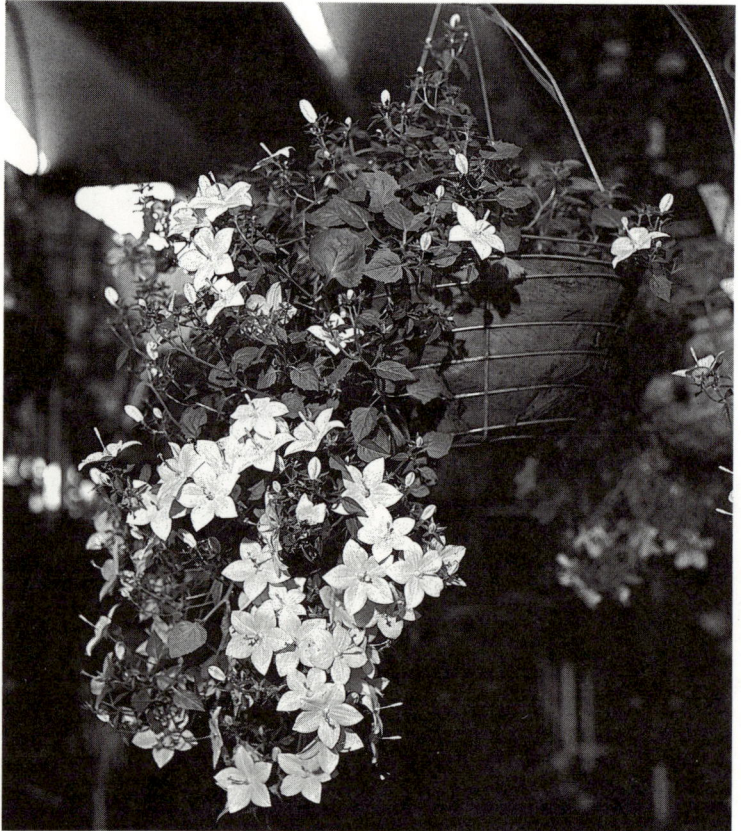

Campanula isophylla A welcome addition to the range of summer flowers suited to basket culture.

Chrysanthemum

B C F J   *

Chrysanthemum The pot-mum is specially grown for indoor decoration.
Keep them moist, cool and in good light.

The potted chrysanthemum is purchased throughout the
year for indoor colour. If you place them in a well–lit
aspect and keep them cool at night, the flowers last for
weeks. The colour range includes white, yellow, pink
and lilac and the bronze tonings. After flowering, plant in
the garden. Propagation is by cuttings.

Clerodendrum   Bleeding heart vine

B D F H   ***

Clerodendrum An eye-catching combination of red, white and green, the
bleeding heart vine needs extra care for success.

The bleeding heart vines are tropical creepers with attractive flowers. *C. thomsonae* has red flowers and white bracts which turn pink. It occasionally produces a turquoise berry. *C. splendens* has dark-red flowers. These are frost tender and usually grown in heated greenhouses or warm sunrooms. Propagation is by cuttings.

Columnea

B D E H　　****** The modern columnea is a first-class house plant. A basket plant in full flower is quite breath-taking. Flowering is intermittent from spring to autumn. The long trailers respond to regular pinching. Regular feeding is beneficial. In unheated rooms, keep dryish over winter. Columneas prefer to be slightly pot-bound. Repot using an African violet mixture. Are attacked by mite. Propagation is by cuttings or seeds.

See colour plates.

Crossandra

B D F H　　******* A small, bright house plant with dark-green foliage and large, orange flowers. Keep them away from direct sunlight. Crossandra needs a light, airy, moist potting mix for its small root system. Some humidity is recommended. With good care, flowering lasts for months. Propagation is by cuttings.

See colour plates.

Cymbidium　　　　　　　Cymbidium orchid

B C F G J PSOME　***** The cymbidium orchid is one of the most popular winter-flowering house plants. The flowering season extends from June to November, and plants are available in a large range of colours. Cymbidiums are an outdoor plant brought into the house for 4 to 6 weeks while in bloom.

　A cool, airy situation is desirable. The flowers quickly age in central-heating or if the plant continually dries out. Repotting occurs after flowering using special orchid composts. Division of the clump is the easiest method of propagation.

Cymbidium orchids *A hardy orchid for the cooler climate, it requires no heat. Bring it inside once the flowers have opened.*

Daphne odora

Daphne is normally grown in the garden, but like the bouvardia and the gardenia, it can be used indoors for a few days at a time. The smallish flowers are exquisitely perfumed. Keep the plant away from heating and mist the foliage. Place it in the cool overnight. Propagation is by cuttings.

B C F J K P   *

Daphne odora *The sweetly perfumed daphne flowers over winter. It grows well in a pot and may be taken indoors for short periods.*

Episcia Flame violet

A D E H　　****** An eye-catching relative of the columnea, with beautiful-ly marked velvety foliage and bright flowers. The flame violet is best grown as a basket plant. Feed regularly from spring to autumn. Are attacked by mite. Propagation is by cuttings or small plantlets.

Episcia Small, eye-catching trailers with beautifully marked leaves and tubular flowers. They like similar conditions to African violets.

86

Erica

Hardy, colourful outdoor shrubs flowering from autumn to spring. They cannot stay indoors permanently, but may be used for short periods in a bright, airy room. They must not dry out, and should be kept away from heating. Prune back after flowering. Propagation is by cuttings.

B C F J   *

Erica A popular house plant in Europe, the heath gives weeks of colour.

Exacum affine

Exacum Masses of dainty, lightly perfumed mauve and gold flowers. A summer annual grown easily by seed.

B D E J P MILD   *

A compact, annual house plant valued for its lilac blue flowers and mild fragrance. Each flower has a gold centre. The fine roots prefer a moist, but airy, growing mixture with good drainage. Some humidity is recommended. They are grown from seeds.

Fuchsia

B C F G J K   *   Fuchsia are easy to grow and flower profusely. There are many hundreds to choose from. They are mainly garden plants and make colourful pot plants, standard specimens or baskets. A fernery, porch or veranda is suitable in very frosty locations. Keep them out of hot, windy areas. The growth is brittle and benefits from regular tip pruning. They should not be kept inside for more than a few days. Feed regularly, but not during winter. Prune in late winter. Watch for aphids, grubs and mite. Fuchsia strikes readily from cuttings.

Fuchsia Careful training and pruning produces a basket that flowers for months.

Gardenia

B C F J K P   *

Gardenia Exquisitely perfumed shrubs. A must for temporary use indoors.

The gardenia grows as a smallish garden plant in southern Australia in frost-free locations. The foliage is a fresh, glossy-green, and the beautifully perfumed flowers open white and fade to gold. Gardenias dislike hot, direct sun and need high humidity. Mist regularly and do not keep indoors for long periods. Mite can be troublesome. Propagation is by cuttings.

Geranium

B C E G J K   *

Geraniums Excellent flowering pot and basket plants requiring minimum attention. Very hardy.

The many varieties of Geranium lend them to pot and basket culture. Tough, colourful plants easy to grow and generous in flowering. Prune as required. Grubs can be troublesome. Easily propagated by cutting.

Hoya   Wax flower

B C E G H J K P ★★ Wax flowers are trailing plants well suited to basket growing. The common hoya, *H. carnosa*, grows in porches with morning sun and frost protection in all but the coldest areas. It bears clusters of pink, star-shaped flowers from spurs which rebloom. The foliage is mid-green and waxy. Some varieties are variegated, and others such as the rope hoya have twisted growth. The miniature hoya, *H. bella*, is bushy and bears masses of scented white and mauve blooms on the new growth. Hoyas must be pot-bound and grow in a well-drained mix. Use only weak doses of fertilizer. Keep them drier in winter. Aphids and mite are the main pests. Propagation is by cuttings or seeds.

Hoya The 'Indian Rope Hoya' has unusual twisted foliage and stems. The pink, waxy flowers are most attractive.

Streptocarpus *The Cape primroses are members of the gesneriad family. They require less heat and grow satisfactorily in a protected porch.*

Cacti and succulents *The unusual appearance and vivid flowers attract many plant fanciers to specialize in these plants.*

Crossandra Glossy deep green foliage and bright apricot flowers are features of this house plant.

BELOW left
Columnea A columnea in full bloom is glorious. They grow successfully at lower temperatures if kept slightly dry.

BELOW Calceolaria The brightness of the calceolaria is cheering in winter. Ideal for an unheated greenhouse.

Ixora

An unusual flowering pot plant usually suitable for the heated greenhouse or the warm, well-lit sunroom. Frost tender. Each growth bears a head of reddish-orange, pink or yellow flowers atop olive-green foliage. Not a plant for cold growing. Propagation is by cuttings.

B D F H   *******

Ixora *Lovely orange-red blooms during the warmer months.*

Kalanchoe

B C E G J   *****

Kalanchoe *These are available in yellow, orange, pink and red. A hardy succulent for a well-lit position.*

The hardy kalanchoe in its many colours is a decorative, easy-to-grow house plant. It is a succulent and requires minimal care. Bright light is essential to keep colour in the flowers. In frost-free areas it can be grown outdoors. Feed regularly until the buds develop. Prune back the old flowering shoots. Easy to propagate by seeds, cuttings or leaves.

Lilium   Lily

B C F J PSOME   ***** There are many bulbs available for temporary use indoors. Lilies are excellent cut flowers, and equally successful pot plants. A plant in full colour is glorious. Move the plant outdoors once the flowers fade. Many are sweetly perfumed. Propagation is by seed and bulblets.

Liliums *The lilium season covers many months. A careful choice of varieties ensures colour from summer to autumn.*

Plumeria   Frangipani

B D E G J P   ******* Frangipani is not the most decorative house plant, but it is beautifully perfumed. It flowers during the summer. Each flower is a pure glistening white with a yellow centre. Red and pink varieties are also grown. During the dormant period, the plant has no leaves and must be kept quite dry. Overwatered plants rot quickly. They have a

Plumeria *Frangipani is grown for its strongly perfumed white and golden yellow flowers. Pink and red forms are also available.*

small and brittle root. Use a quick-draining potting mix. Mite is troublesome in hot stuffy conditions. Propagation is by cuttings.

Senecio cruentus

Cineraria

B C E G J   **∗**

Senecio cruentus *The popular annual cineraria may be brought indoors for short periods. Plant them in autumn.*

The Cineraria is a charming annual for winter and spring colour to brighten the fernery, porch or living area. The flower is of daisy shape and is usually two-toned. Blues, pinks and dusky reds are the main colours. Culture is similar to Calceolaria. Propagation is by seed.

Sinningia pusilla
'Doll Baby'

B D F H　　******　　Doll Baby is a mini-gloxinia with dainty foxglove-like flowers and soft patterned leaves. The flower is lilac mauve and white. Grow them as you would gloxinias. Ideal for a terrarium. Propagation is by seed or leaf cutting.

Sinningia pusilla 'Doll Baby' A miniature gesneriad with soft foliage and single lavender and white flowers. Good for terrariums.

Stephanotis

B D F H P　　*******　　A fast-growing vine with dark-green foliage similar to the Hoya, and clusters of highly-scented, white blooms in summer. A difficult plant to grow for those without winter heat — it is a frost tender plant. The stephanotis needs high humidity and a moist growing mix. It can be propagated by seeds or cuttings.

Stephanotis A vigorous summer flowering climber with masses of white, scented flowers.

FLOWERING HOUSE PLANT GUIDE

THE PLANTS listed have been described previously. Many are used indoors on a temporary basis only, preferring to grow outdoors in the garden, porch, fernery and unheated greenhouse. They are returned there or discarded after flowering.

Others need the protected environment of the home for success in a cool climate. The most suitable environment for each is indicated. The flowering times are approximate and will vary regionally.

The Chrysanthemum and Poinsettia are specialist crops bought in flower for temporary decoration, and discarded once flowering ceases.

Those varieties marked intermittent have no definite blooming season.

CODE KEY

SUITABLE ENVIRONMENT

G unheated greenhouse
H permanent indoor growing
J only temporary indoor use
K fernery

BOTANICAL NAME	COMMON NAME	SUITABLE ENVIRONMENT				FLOWERING SEASON			
		G	H	J	K	Sp	Su	Au	W
Achimenes	Hot water plant		■				■	■	
Aeschynanthus	Lipstick plant		■			INTERMITTENT			
Anthurium scherzerianum	Flamingo flower		■			■	■		■
Aphelandra squarrosa	Zebra plant		■			INTERMITTENT			
Azalea				■	■	■		■	■
Begonia elatior	Rieger begonia		■			INTERMITTENT			
Begonia tuberous		■		■			■	■	
Boronia megastigma	Brown boronia			■		■			
Bougainvillea		■		■			■		
Bouvardia				■			■	■	
Bromeliads	Vase plants		■			INTERMITTENT			
Browallia		■		■			■		
Cacti and succulents		■	■	■	■	INTERMITTENT			
Calceolaria		■		■		■			
Camellia				■	■	■		■	■
Campanula isophylla	Italian bellflower	■		■	■		■		
Chrysanthemum				■		ALL YEAR ROUND			
Clerodendrum	Bleeding heart vine		■				■		
Columnea			■	■		INTERMITTENT			
Crossandra			■				■		
Cyclamen persicum		■		■	■			■	■
Cymbidium	Cymbidium orchid	■		■		■			■
Daphne odora				■	■	■			■
Episcia	Flame violet		■			■	■		

BOTANICAL NAME	COMMON NAME	SUITABLE ENVIRONMENT				FLOWERING SEASON			
		G	H	J	K	Sp	Su	Au	W
Erica	Heath			■		■		■	■
Euphorbia	Poinsettia		■			ALL YEAR ROUND			
Exacum affine				■			■	■	
Fuchsia		■		■	■	■	■	■	
Gardenia				■	■	■	■	■	
Geranium		■		■	■	■	■	■	
Hoya	Wax flower	■	■	■	■	■	■		
Impatiens	Busy lizzie	■		■	■	■	■	■	
Ixora			■				■		
Kalanchoe		■		■		■			
Lilium	Lily			■			■	■	
Plumeria	Frangipani	■		■			■		
Primula	Polyanthus	■		■	■				■
	Primrose	■		■	■				■
	P. malacoides	■		■	■				■
	P. obconica	■		■	■	■		■	■
Saintpaulia ionantha	African violet		■			INTERMITTENT			
Senecio cruentus	Cineraria	■		■		■			■
Sinningia pusilla	'Doll Baby'		■				■	■	
Sinningia speciosa	Gloxinia	■	■				■	■	
Spathiphyllum	Madonna lily		■			INTERMITTENT			
Stephanotis			■				■		
Streptocarpus	Cape primrose		■			■	■	■	

FLOWERING HOUSE PLANT GUIDE

COMMON FOLIAGE house plants are included in this section. Those listed first are described in detail, each including an easy care guide, and in alphabetical order of botanical names. Brief descriptions of other important foliage plants follow, also in alphabetical order of botanical names.

Like the flowering house plants, a code is included for each plant to show its main cultural requirements. These codes correspond to the House Plant Guide included at the end of the book.

CODE KEY

LIGHT LEVELS

A low to medium light levels
B medium to bright filtered light

TEMPERATURE

C cool, minimum 7°C at night
D warm, minimum 15°C at night

WATER REQUIREMENTS

E water thoroughly, allow to dry (not completely) between waterings
F keep evenly moist

SUITABLE ENVIRONMENT

G unheated greenhouse
H permanent indoor growing
J only temporary indoor use
K fernery

SPECIAL FEATURE

P perfumed

HARDINESS RATING

* easy to grow, very hardy
** medium-to-easy to grow, hardy
*** difficult to grow, requires extra care

FOLIAGE
HOUSE
PLANTS

Adiantum — Maidenhair ferns

EASY CARE GUIDE

LIGHT No direct sun, plenty of bright filtered light. Some species have specific needs.

TEMPERATURE 8 to 20°C, optimal 10 to 18°C.

WATERING Evenly moist but not saturated. Basket plants need extra care.

HUMIDITY Essential in warm aspects. Mist daily in hot weather.

FEEDING Weak doses regularly to give 'a little often'. Forced soft growth is less durable. Apply slow-release types with care.

AIR General air movement without draughts is beneficial.

REPOTTING Year-round using a well-drained, humus-rich mixture. Keep crown at soil level.

GENERAL CARE Snap off the dead fronds close to the crown. Turn the plant every week to encourage balanced development.

Adiantum fragrans The flowing softness of a well-grown maidenhair complements any home.

Aphids, scale, slugs and
snails, mealy bug.
Botrytis.
PROPAGATION By division
or spores.
Division Late winter. The
rhizomatous species are
suitable for division.
Remove the plant from the
pot and cut the root-ball
into good sized wedges
each having plenty of
roots and stems. Very
small pieces may not
survive. Repot each
wedge into fresh mix and
water thoroughly. *Note:*
The majority of maidenhair
in cultivation, e.g. *A.
fragrans, A. elegans*, grow
from congested crowns
which rarely divide
successfully. Propagate
these by spore.
Spore Spring to autumn.
Fern spore is fine and
dust-like. It is
exceptionally buoyant and
must be sown indoors
and away from draughts.
A constantly moist
medium is essential for
germination. Shallow food
containers are ideal
propagators. Half fill the
tray with finely-sieved
medium, firm and
moisten. Drain off the
excess water. Tap the
spore lightly over the mix
and seal. Locate in a light
position but away from the
sun. Once the spore
germinates and the true
leaves emerge, open the
lid gradually to admit
some air and harden-off
the sporelings. A careful
watch of moisture levels at
this point is vital. Gradually
move them into more light
as they grow. Transplant
the clumps of sporelings

AMONG THE many house plants, few match the fresh green fronds of the maidenhair for lending elegance and softness to the home. Plants come in an amazing assortment of shapes and sizes. Some of the more tropical species have large bold leaves, while others from cooler zones are small and delicate; with countless variations in between.

The majority enjoy good levels of light with adequate humidity and some air movement. There are those that prefer less light, notably the finer forms with very thin leaflets. The leaflets have a low resistance to concentrated heat and dehydrate rapidly, irrespective of soil moisture. Sunlight shining directly onto the plant results in severe yellowing and stunting or burning.

No maidenhair revels in hot stuffiness and they seldom live in air-conditioned or heated rooms for very long. High temperatures are not essential and many grow happily in a cool veranda or living area. If the position is unsuitable, the leaves develop brown edges and the new fronds may shrivel or be lank and drawn. Low temperatures produce stronger and sturdier plants. Maidenhair thrives with plenty of fresh air or general air circulation. Draughts, hot or cold, are to be avoided. In summer, a hot northerly wind will destroy an unprotected plant and those in hanging containers are at greatest risk.

An even supply of moisture is essential, although the frequency of application does vary with the season and climate. Lack-lustre foliage may be the outcome of too much water which saturates the soil and kills the fine feeder roots. Ensure that all drainage water is emptied out of saucers (including hanging pots) during the cooler months. Maidenhair is tolerant of a little dryness but not for very long. The self-watering pot provides a straightforward and effective method of watering ferns. Naturally plants grown in very good light use more food, but even so feeding must be tailored to plant response. The seaweed fertilizers are particularly well suited. A small top dressing of slow-release fertilizer once or twice a year is satisfactory.

The maidenhair is a low maintenance plant. Apart from removing the spent fronds, all that is required is a monthly shower and a daily misting during the hot weather.

Occasionally the foliage becomes tired-looking all at once. Take the opportunity to clean away the old stems and cut it back to just above the crown. The new fronds will then grow without hindrance. Dried-out plants are treated similarly and will respond if the roots and growing points have not been damaged beyond repair.

The new fronds of the adiantum may be red, pink, brown or green according to variety and the cultural conditions. *Adiantum fragrans* which is the most popular and best variety for indoor use is green irrespective of treatment. *A. elegans* and *A. micropinnulum* by contrast are brownish-orange to pink, the depth of tone altering with the amount of heat, nutrition and light the plant receives. A healthy frond is soft and springy to the touch; a dying one shrivelled and brittle.

Maidenhair makes a superb specimen either in a pot or basket, or as part of a mixed planting. The extensive number of varieties provides ample scope for success in the fernery or greenhouse, and indoors. In the southern regions of Australia, *Adiantum fragrans* is hard to surpass for interior decoration. The foliage is a fresh green carried on contrasting brownish stems. It does well in medium- to well-lit aspects and is tolerant of bright light. The plant has a sturdy compact habit and grows outdoors given proper protection. Other varieties that perform successfully indoors are *A. elegans*, *A.* 'Fritz Luthii' and *A. micropinnulum*.

Regular repotting of young plants keeps them growing without interruption, while older plants will continue to thrive in the one sized container given adequate feeding. Repotting established plants should commence before the spring flush of growth to minimize disturbance. The crown is best kept at the same level or fractionally deeper if it wobbles. If it is buried too deeply it may not survive.

Maidenhair has a fair share of pests, and one disease of concern, botrytis, causes leaf browning and matting in still, humid conditions such as occur when the pots are kept close together. By spacing the pots to increase air movement, this problem normally disappears. Greenhouse culture can be tricky over the winter, when ventilation is infrequent and the humidity builds up. A small circulating fan will stir the air and discourage botrytis.

Slugs and snails hide among the foliage, the crown and in the drainage holes. Together with aphids, they destroy or damage the young fronds and require control before numbers build up. Aphids are especially troublesome and will change colour to blend in with the host plant. Scale is

into individual tubes or space them in trays for growing on.

101

sometimes confused with the spore-bearing vessels located on the undersides of each frond. Spore patterns are consistent on each plant although they differ from species to species. Scale, however, is random in distribution, and is characterized by a sticky secretion and often accompanied by sooty mould.

Aglaonema Chinese lucky plant

A D F H   *

EASY CARE GUIDE

LIGHT Dull to well-lit; no direct sunlight. Artificial sources are satisfactory.
TEMPERATURE 10 to 30°C, optimal 15 to 20°C. Reduce water and food in cool and dark places.
WATERING Moist, not wet; drier in winter. Tolerates periods of dryness; however, leaves die prematurely if the plant is too dry.
HUMIDITY Will tolerate dry atmospheres. To create extra humidity, sit the pot on a saucer filled with pebbles which are kept wet. The pot must not sit in water.
FEEDING Responds well to fertilizers given during the growing season.
REPOTTING Annual repotting is unnecessary but beneficial. A moist, well-drained, humus-rich potting mix is preferred. Choose a pot only one to two sizes larger, as the root system is small.
PESTS AND DISEASES Aphids, scale and mealy bug. Root rot.

Aglaonema commutatum 'Treubii' *The colourful aglaonema thrives in poorly lit situations.*

THE CHINESE lucky plant, *Aglaonema*, is a surprisingly tough house plant which adapts readily to difficult conditions. It is tolerant of general neglect, poor light and erratic watering. It is a native to south-east Asia where it lives on the forest floor in well-drained, humus-rich soils.

102

The aglaonema has unusual pale-green, lily-like flowers and often produces an attractive orange-red berry. The foliage is thick, leathery and durable, and able to withstand periods of dryness, and air-conditioning.

Two varieties, *A. commutatum* and *A. modestum*, are especially durable and are often used for particularly dull areas. The colour range is quite extensive including the plainer greens of *A. commutatum* and *A. modestum*, and the more unusual silvery tonings of *A.* 'Pewter' and *A.* 'Silver Queen'. *A. pseudo-bracteatum* is a vigorous variety with light-green foliage liberally splashed with yellow and cream. The more highly coloured varieties prefer better light.

Little maintenance is required apart from cleaning, watering and feeding. Any straggly stems may be pruned back to stimulate new growth lower down. They multiply readily from suckers and soon form bushy clumps.

PROPAGATION Cuttings, division and seed in spring.

Division Remove well-developed suckers and pot into small pots. Place in a warm, shaded spot and cover with plastic until established. Gradually harden-off.

Cuttings Cut pieces 10 to 18 cm long and remove the lower two-thirds of the leaves. Dip into a hormone striking powder. Insert into a standard three part sand to one part peatmoss mixture, firm, water in and place in a warm, shaded room. Cover with plastic, inspect daily for watering. Remove any flowers or dead leaves. Use fungicides to control rot if necessary. Harden-off before potting into small containers.

Seed Collect the ripe seed and sow immediately into a well-drained propagating mixture. Cover lightly and water. Keep in a warm position and water as required. Once the leaves emerge give more light. Pot into tubes when large enough to handle.

Aglaonema commutatum One of the many Chinese lucky plants noted for their hardiness in southern Australia.

Cissus

A B C E H K ★★

EASY CARE GUIDE

LIGHT Plenty of filtered bright light. In poor light growth is slower and less vigorous. Direct sunlight results in scorching.

TEMPERATURE 12 to 30°C, optimal 18°C. Ensure adequate air circulation in hot weather, misting foliage daily to increase humidity. Avoid draughts.

WATERING *Cissus* are very sensitive to overwatering and cold soggy soils. Keep moist during the growing season; drier in winter. Never leave the pot sitting in water.

FEEDING Spring to late summer. Leaf chlorosis may result if plants are overfed. Slow-release fertilizers supplemented by a seaweed product are satisfactory.

REPOTTING Early spring to mid-autumn. A moist, humus-rich, well-drained potting mix is essential. The root system is small and big containers are necessary. Avoid root disturbance.

GENERAL CARE Cleaning dust from the leaves. Training and tip-pruning of the new growth.

PESTS AND DISEASES Aphids, mite and mealy bug. Powdery mildew.

PROPAGATION Difficult for the home gardener, but worth a try. A source of bottom heat to keep the cuttings at 20 to 24°C is desirable. Use hardened pieces, 5 to 10 cm long, from which the soft tips

Cissus A durable foliage plant for baskets and totem poles.

THE GRAPE ivy family, *Cissus*, includes two excellent varieties that grow satisfactorily in either dull or well-lit aspects. One is the original species, *C. rhombifolia*, the other a superior and more vigorous sport (developed in Denmark), *C.* 'Ellen Danica'. *C. rhombifolia* has attractive three-part, glossy, dark-green leaves that are lightly toothed. Each new leaf and shoot is covered by a silvery down. 'Ellen Danica' retains the basic form with each leaflet boldly incised and slightly larger. They are both fast-growing climbers with tendrils that wrap around suitable surfaces for support.

The grape ivy is displayed best as a hanging basket or totem pole specimen. The training of these shoots entails weaving them around and through each other so that the basket and its hangers, or the totem pole, is completely covered. After the basic framework is in place, frequent tip-pruning of the shoots helps to fill out the plant.

For all its hardiness, the grape ivy dislikes hot, stuffy conditions. Badly affected plants loose their lustre with many of the new leaves drying-off. Baskets grown close to the ceiling in heated rooms are especially vulnerable. Remove them to a cooler location and cut back the bare stems to healthy leaves.

You may successfully grow the *Cissus* in well-protected porches and ferneries in southern Australia. But be prepared to give ample frost protection and for growth to yellow during the cooler months.

and the leaves from the bottom half of the cutting have been removed. Dip in a liquid hormone striking medium and insert in a moist mix of three parts propagating sand or perlite to one part peatmoss. Firm and water well. Cover with a plastic bag and set in a warmish, well-lit spot. Inspect daily, water as needed, remove any dead material. Once struck, gradually harden-off before potting two or three cuttings to a 10 cm pot.

Codiaeum Croton

CROTONS, WITHOUT doubt, have the most beautifully coloured foliage of all house plants. The colour range combines reds, oranges, browns, yellows and greens in many and varied patterns. The leaf shapes show remarkable variations, with twists, spirals, wavy margins and trident formations. The brilliance and depth of colour of the leaf develops best in bright light. Many begin as green and yellow, gradually developing the change and intensity of colour as they mature.

Winter is the danger period for crotons in southern Australia. They will not survive sustained periods of cold, including frost, and so require a minimum temperature of around 15°C. Below this the older foliage drops, growth ceases and the plant loses condition. If, however, the growing mix is kept drier, new growth can be expected once the weather warms. A light pruning back to healthy foliage in spring soon produces vigorous new growth.

Rejuvenating old specimens devoid of bottom leaves can be complicated. If they are cut back too severely, they die. Air layering is one solution to this problem, and is carried out in late spring. This method works equally well on young plants, and is the easiest method of propagation for the home enthusiast.

Crotons resent prolonged dryness and some leaf drop is inevitable. Beware of overwatering and ensure drainage is adequate.

B D F H ★★★

EASY CARE GUIDE

LIGHT Bright, but with no direct sunlight during the summer.
TEMPERATURE 15 to 30°C. Below 15°C some deterioration may occur. Frost sensitive. Suitable for heated greenhouses.
WATERING Use tepid water. Keep moist at all times, but drier in cooler situations and where growth stops during winter.
HUMIDITY Crotons appreciate a humid atmosphere which assists in the control of red spider mite.
FEEDING Spring and autumn. Slow-release fertilizers are suitable.

REPOTTING Spring to early autumn. Crotons have small root systems and tolerate being root-bound for some time. A well-draining mixture that holds adequate moisture is satisfactory.

GENERAL CARE Sponge down and remove dust from foliage regularly. Occasional pruning of leggy growth.

PESTS AND DISEASES Mite, scale, mealy bug and aphids. Root rot.

PROPAGATION Spring and summer by cuttings and air layering.

Cuttings Select a piece of current season's growth around 10 cm long that has hardened-up. Remove the lower two-thirds of the foliage, dip the base in a hormone rooting powder and insert the cutting in propagating mix. Firm and water. Cover with a plastic bag and keep in a warm, well-lit room. A bottom temperature of 20 to 24°C is desirable. Gradually toughen-up the cutting once roots form before potting-up.

Air layering Enclose a section of bare stem with a wad of moist sphagnum moss. Wrap this with plastic film and tie securely around the top, the bottom, and the middle to exclude air. Use a clear film so that you can see the new roots easily. Cut the layer from the parent once the moss is full of roots, and carefully remove the plastic film. Pot into a clean container without disturbing the moss. Enclose the top in a plastic bag with some air holes until the plant is established. Slowly accustom the plant to the room environment.

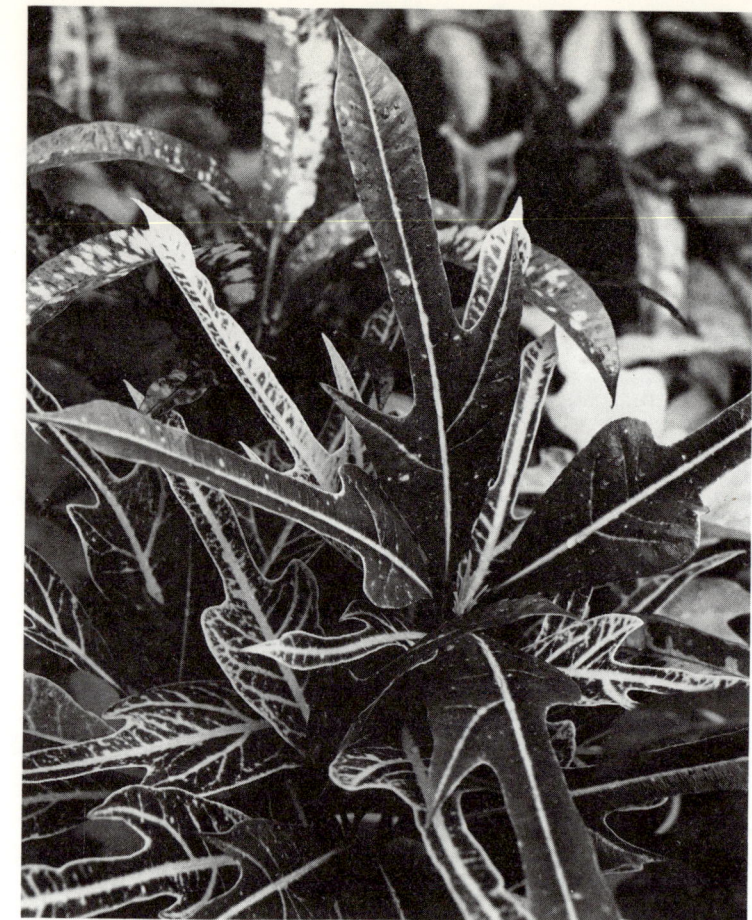

Codiaeum Spectacular, colourful foliage and sturdy growth.

Dieffenbachia   Dumb cane

B D F H   *******   *DIEFFENBACHIA* IS a bold–leaved house plant noted for its delightful tonings of green and gold; and a tolerance to heat and bright light. The common name, dumb cane, arises because its sap may cause a swelling of the tongue and temporary speech loss. Because of this, particular care must be taken when young children are around.

Codiaeum The crotons are hard to better
for brilliantly toned foliage. They thrive
in warm, bright rooms.

Adiantum fragrans *A superb maidenhair fern appreciative of good light and a cool, airy position.*

Cissus *Grape ivies are excellent house plants for either dull or well-lit rooms. Train and prune the young growth regularly.*

Dieffenbachia Does well in heated conditions, and is suitable for hydroculture.

Dieffenbachias must have warmth in winter to maintain them in good condition. If plants are cold, they cease growing and shed their bottom leaves. You can lessen the effects of coldness to some extent by keeping the soil drier. The brightly variegated varieties, such as *D*. 'Camille', *D*. 'Galaxy' and *D*. 'Exotica Compacta', produce their best colour in bright light. Other less-variegated forms may develop leaf yellowing where the light is too strong.

Adequate humidity is advisable in high temperatures to prevent browning of the leaf edges. Dieffenbachias appreciate humidity and thrive in hydroculture.

Throughout the winter period pay particular attention to watering. The Dieffenbachia resents a cold and soggy growing medium.

EASY CARE GUIDE

LIGHT Dull to well-lit. In poor light, growth will be slow; in such conditions the predominantly green varieties will do better.
TEMPERATURE 15 to 30°C, optimal 18 to 25°C.
WATERING Use tepid water only. Keep moist during the growing season; drier in winter. Overdryness may cause early leaf death. Never sit pots in water.
HUMIDITY High or low levels are acceptable. In hot, stuffy rooms adequate levels are essential. Mist the foliage and sit the pot on a saucer of moist pebbles.
FEEDING Spring to autumn. Dieffenbachias are gross feeders, especially in heated conditions. Feed as indicated by plant response, using a well-balanced fertilizer. Seaweed and fish types are excellent.
REPOTTING Spring to early autumn, using a well-drained, humus-rich potting mix. Repot every 12 to 18 months or as needed. Avoid root disturbance. Set the plants slightly deeper in the new container.

GENERAL CARE A monthly shower to remove any dust. Old leaves are cut off at the stem and the stump allowed to dry completely before removal is attempted. Give plants growing near a window a quarter-turn weekly to encourage balanced development.

PESTS AND DISEASES Mealy bug, aphids and mite. Root rot.
PROPAGATION Spring and summer by cuttings and air layering.
Air layering Select a strong growth. Wrap a generous wad of moist sphagnum moss around the bare stem and enclose with plastic. Tie securely top and bottom. Support the layered stem with a stake to prevent it snapping off. Sever the new plant from its parent once a strong root-ball develops. Carefully remove the plastic and pot-up. Water well place in a warm, shaded spot.

Cuttings Remove the leaves from the lower half of a healthy cutting 15 to 20 cm long, and insert into propagating mix. Firm, water thoroughly and enclose the cutting in a plastic bag. Place in a warm spot. Once growth begins gradually harden-off before potting.

Dizygotheca elegantissima   Finger aralia

B D E H   ★★★

EASY CARE GUIDE

LIGHT Plenty of filtered light; avoid all direct sunlight. Turn plants regularly for balanced growth. In poor light growth may cease.

TEMPERATURE 16 to 30°C. At high temperatures, air circulation (not a draught) is beneficial. The finger aralia is seldom happy in temperatures below 16°C.

WATERING Use only tepid water, keeping evenly moist but not wet. In winter soils should stay just moist. The dizygotheca does not use a lot of water.

FEEDING Regular applications during the growing season. Avoid high nitrogen formulations. Do not feed in winter.

REPOTTING Spring to early autumn. The dizygotheca has a small, weak root system which is the cause of most problems. To overcome this, avoid root disturbance and only repot when plants are pot-bound. Quite large plants will grow in small pots, for example, a 60 cm plant in a 12 to 15 cm pot. Use a light mix rich in organic matter with excellent drainage.

PESTS AND DISEASES Mealy bug, scale, mite and aphids. Root rot.

Dizygotheca As an accent plant the finger aralia is most effective.

THE SUPERB finger aralia, *Dizygotheca elegantissima*, is an outstanding house plant with palmate, metallic brown-green foliage borne on elegant stems. The feathery foliage is seen to best advantage against light backgrounds as an accent or specimen plant. Multiheaded specimens are quite striking and can be created either by planting an odd number of young plants together, or by tip-pruning at an early stage.

The finger aralia will grow in cooler climates with winter warmth. It reacts quickly to wet feet by shedding its bottom-most leaves, exposing ugly sections of bare stem. The dizygotheca exhibits its dislike of uncongenial conditions through drooping and lack-lustre foliage, pinched or stagnant growth, and brown leaf tips. In most cases an adjustment to the watering regime or shifting to a new location helps. During the hotter months and in the winter with artificial heating, a regular spray over the leaves using tepid water is recommended.

Older plants with bare stems will reshoot when cut back to two to three healthy leaves. It is safer to prune only one stem at a time, thus allowing each to grow away vigorously before cutting another.

PROPAGATION By seeds and cuttings.

Seeds Fresh seed is essential. Sow in a well-drained mix in spring with bottom heat of 22 to 24°C. Pot good-sized seedlings into tubes, being careful not to damage the small, weak roots. Pot into large pots once established.

Cuttings Use current season's growth that is firm. Select 15 cm long pieces and remove leaves on the lower half to two-thirds. Firm into moist sphagnum moss or propagating medium, water and cover with a plastic bag. Place in a warm, well-lit position. Bottom heat of 20 to 24°C ensures speedy root production. Pot-on when established.

Dracaena

Dracaena Hardy, durable house plants noted for their decorative foliage.   **B D F H P**SOME   ✶✶

LIGHT Dull to well-lit. Bleaching and burning occurs in direct or excessive light.

TEMPERATURE 15 to 30°C, optimal 15 to 20°C.

WATERING Keep moist; drier in winter. Keep water off the foliage during the winter, especially in unheated areas.

HUMIDITY Regular misting will assist in combating leaf fatigue.

FEEDING Spring to autumn with a well-balanced fertilizer. Do not feed during winter. Plants in low light positions are fed less frequently.

REPOTTING Spring to late summer. Dracaenas flourish in a humus-rich soil with excellent drainage. Repot as soon as growth shows signs of stagnating.

GENERAL CARE Regular cleaning of the foliage is beneficial. Keep an eye out for insect pests at the same time. Old leaves should be cut off flush, and the base allowed to dry completely before any attempt is made to remove it.

PESTS AND DISEASES
Aphids, mite, scale and mealy bug.

PROPAGATION By air layering and cuttings.
Air layers The best method for the home enthusiast. Carefully remove the leaves from a section of stem approximately 15 cm long and enclose this area with a wad of moist sphagnum moss. Wrap with clear plastic, and tie securely

Dracaena godseffiana 'Milky Way' *Superb golden yellow and green glossy foliage.*

THE DRACAENAS are a hardy group of tropical palm-like plants suitable for indoor use in cooler climates. Some species require more heat than others and you will find it worthwhile to keep this in mind when choosing between varieties.

All species appreciate well-lit conditions, especially the variegated varieties such as *D. fragrans* 'Lindenii', *D. f.* 'Massangeana' and *D. godseffiana*. The plainer types are more tolerant of poor light although growth is much slower — these include *D. deremensis*, *D. fragrans* and *D. marginata*. There are two main groups divided according to their habit of growth — the tree types and the bushy, suckering types. The tree types are shown to best advantage as shaped or multistemmed specimens. The broad, glossy foliage of *D. fragrans* is ideal for this treatment, with both *D. deremensis* and *D. marginata* and their varieties equally as effective.

D. fragrans 'Massangeana' will be known to many as the Chinese happy plant. A section of bare stem is placed into a bowl of pebbles where it forms roots and produces new shoots. The roots are kept moist at all times, with the regular addition of fully soluble fertilizer to supply essential nutrients.

The bushy, suckering types, such as *D. godseffiana* and *D. surculosa*, are rhizomatous. The thin new shoots arise from beneath the soil level to form a clump. The foliage is arranged in circles or whorls at intervals along the canes. The leaves tend to be thick and leathery which makes them better able to withstand air dryness. *D. godseffiana* has two beautiful varieties — 'Milky Way', dark-green with a creamy-gold band, and 'Florida Beauty', freely splashed with creamy yellow.

top and bottom. The layer is severed from the parent once the new roots have formed. Gently remove the plastic and pot-up, disturbing the root-ball as little as possible.
Cuttings Spring and summer. Select a cutting 30 cm long and remove leaves for one-quarter to one-third up from the base. Dip in hormone rooting powder and place in a propagating mix of one part peat and one part perlite. Maintain a temperature of 25°C. Pot into larger containers once the plant is growing vigorously.

Epipremnum aureus Devil's ivy

THE HALLMARK of a first-class house plant is its popularity. The devil's ivy has been cultivated for many years and has proven itself to be hardy, durable and adaptable to indoor conditions. The devil's ivy has had a number of name changes. You may know it better as Pothos, Scindapsus or Rapidophora. It originates in the Solomon Islands as a strong epiphytic vine with large, glossy green and gold foliage. There are a number of varieties including 'Marble Queen', a creamy yellow and green, and 'Goldilocks', a lime gold.

Leaf colour is variable depending upon light intensity. Highly-coloured plants lose their variegation and become predominantly green if placed in dull positions. Conversely, the new leaves on plants relocated in a brighter room show an increase in the amount of gold. As a guide, choose plants showing plenty of gold on the stems and foliage because plants with green stems seldom produce good colour.

Devil's ivy rates highly on the hardiness scale, being in the same class as *Philodendron cordatum* and the *Spathiphyllum*. It takes fluctuating light, temperature and water

A B D E H   *****

EASY CARE GUIDE

LIGHT Bright to poorly lit; filtered light or artificial sources. Both varieties 'Marble Queen' and 'Goldilocks' dislike very bright conditions. No direct sunlight.
TEMPERATURE 12°C to 30°C, optimal 18°C. Plants survive in the cool provided the soil is dryish.
WATERING Keep moist, not wet; drier in winter. Use tepid water and empty the saucers of all drainage. Overwatered plants start yellowing from the base rapidly. Dryness is evident by wilting and loss of the occasional leaf.

111

FEEDING Spring to
autumn. *E. aureus*
responds to heavy
feeding, although it is
quite content with less
feeding. Slow-release and
seaweed-type fertilizers
are recommended. Leaf
tip burning may occur if
the plants are overfed, or
are fed while dry.

REPOTTING Spring to
autumn. While annual
repotting is not needed,
root-bound plants grow
poorly. Repot into the next
sized container using a
well-drained mixture.
Keep root disturbance to
a minimum.

GENERAL CARE A monthly
shower to keep the foliage
free of dust and looking
good. Train and tie the
stems regularly. Mist daily
in summer and when
heating is on.

PESTS AND DISEASES
Mealy bug and aphids.
Root rot.

PROPAGATION By cuttings
in spring to autumn. Tip
cuttings should be firm
and approximately 10 cm
long and stem cuttings
should have two to three
nodes. Firm into a moist
mixture of three parts
perlite (or sand) to one
part peatmoss (or
vermiculite). Cover with a
plastic bag and place
where a temperature of
15°C is maintained. Pot
into small tubes once
established.

Epipremnum *The Devil's ivy is tolerant of all but the coldest of conditions.
A strong growing vine ideal for a basket or totem pole.*

levels within its stride. Overwatering is the commonest
cause of failure. It is important that plants dry out *slightly*
between waterings, and be kept drier in winter.

Warmth during the colder months is beneficial,
although devil's ivy will survive at temperatures of 10°C.
Some leaf drop may occur if cold-grown plants are kept
too moist.

Devil's ivy is adaptable to the various styles of growing. It makes a handsome totem or basket plant, and
looks superb trained along a bookcase, the wall, or across
the ceiling. The totem pole allows the plant to adopt its
climbing habit to produce a column of colour that is ideal
for restricted spaces. A long-lasting and sturdy support is
advisable. All plant ties should be checked and adjusted
during routine care.

It is not difficult to grow your own thick, lush hanging
basket. Set a number of young plants together in the
centre of a basket and train the shoots around the top
before allowing them to trail. Regular tip-pruning
encourages extra bushiness. Whenever plastic baskets are
used, take extra care with watering. The soil dries out
more slowly and may remain wet for too long. Devil's
ivy dislikes cold wet soil.

Fatshedera lizei

Fatshedera A tall, fast grower for the fernery, porch or cool-room indoors. It requires staking and tying for support.

FATSHEDERA LIZEI was developed from a cross between the Irish ivy and the house aralia (*Fatsia japonica* 'Moseri') during 1921. It has broad, light to dark green foliage carried on vigorous upright stems that need some support. There are a number of varieties available, including *F. I. undulata*, with larger leaves with wavy edges; *F. I. variegata*, a delightful cream sport which prefers unheated conditions; and *F. I.* 'Pia' which has gold and green tonings.

A C F G H K   ∗

EASY CARE GUIDE

LIGHT Dull to moderate levels; no direct sunlight. Bright rooms with protection from direct sun are suitable provided high temperatures are not maintained for long periods.

TEMPERATURE 7 to 25°C, optimal 15°C. Fresh air is always beneficial, especially during hot spells.

WATERING Keep moist at all times, especially during hot weather.

HUMIDITY Essential (together with fresh air) in hot stuffy rooms. Mist the foliage regularly.

FEEDING Fatshedera responds well to regular weak applications during the spring to autumn seasons. Reduce the frequency if growth becomes too soft and sappy. Do not feed during dormancy.

REPOTTING Spring to autumn. Regular repotting is not needed with established plants. Young plants will need to be repotted once they become pot-bound. The potting mix should have plenty of organic matter and drain well.

PESTS AND DISEASES Mite, scale, mealy bug and aphids. Root rot.

PROPAGATION All year by
cuttings and air layering.
Cuttings In water or
propagating mixture.
Semi-hard cuttings are
best. Remove the leaves
from the bottom half of the
cutting, dip in hormone
rooting powder and insert
firmly into the propagating
medium. Water well and
place in a cool spot.
Cuttings are potted, either
singly or in groups, once
the roots are growing
vigorously.
Air layering Remove the
leaves from a 15 cm
section of stem. Enclose
this with a well-moistened
wad of sphagnum moss.
Wrap carefully in plastic
and tie the top, middle
and bottom securely to
retain the moisture. The
new plant is cut from the
parent plant and potted
up once the new roots are
well developed.

The fatshedera exhibits the same hardiness for cool,
dull situations as its parents. It grows particularly well in
unheated rooms — an advantage in the control of mite
and is an ideal fernery or garden plant.

When grown in warm areas indoors, the young
growth often becomes stressed and limp. This condition
normally passes as the leaves mature but you should,
however, maintain plenty of soil moisture when growth
is active.

The fatshedera makes a striking specimen either singly
or as a group planting around a bamboo stake. To grow
your own multiplant specimen, select an odd number of
strongly growing cuttings, say five to seven, for a 20 cm
pot. Arrange these around a sturdy stake and gently fill
the pot with an indoor potting mixture. Under no circumstances plant the cuttings first and push the stake in
afterwards — the roots and stems will be damaged. Support the shoots as they grow using a flexible material such
as wool or ribbon. Plastic tie material which incorporates
metal is convenient but must be checked regularly to
prevent constriction and possible 'snapping off' of the
stem.

Grafting is not a common practice with house plants,
however the vigour of the fatshedera makes it ideal.
Strong growths are trained to the desired height and,
during late winter, ivy is grafted onto these using the
cleft method. The result is an exceptionally attractive
weeping standard. The smaller, closer-noded varieties,
for example 'Adam', 'Glacier' and 'Pittsburgh', develop
compact heads that respond to tip-pruning.

Ficus benjamina   Weeping fig

B D F H   ★★

EASY CARE GUIDE

LIGHT Low to well-lit; no
direct sun. Growth at low
light levels is slow and
spindly.
TEMPERATURE 15 to 30°C,
optimal 18 to 25°C.

THE *FICUS* are a decorative group of foliage house plants
that are adapted well to the indoor climate. Previously
the popular India rubber tree, *Ficus elastica*, was the most
widely grown of the genus. The graceful beauty of the
weeping fig, *Ficus benjamina*, has now replaced it as one
of the top house plants.

The weeping fig is a small tree from tropical Asia with
overlapping mid-green leaves on thin pendulous
branches. *F b.* 'Exotica' is a superior form with slightly
wavy and shiny foliage. It is better suited to the home

Ficus benjamina *The weeping fig lends an air of elegance to the home.*

WATERING Keep moist, allowing to dry slightly between waterings. Use tepid water at all times.
HUMIDITY Essential in heating and hot weather. Mist daily.
FEEDING Spring to early autumn. Regular weak doses of fertilizer.
REPOTTING Spring to autumn with a moist, but well-draining, mix. Do not disturb the roots. Keep slightly pot-bound.
GENERAL CARE Regular cleaning of the foliage. Prune the leading shoots to produce a bushier and stronger plant. Young plants are often staked and tied. Adjust and remove the stakes once the main stems are self-supporting.
PESTS AND DISEASES Mite and mealy bug. Root rot.
PROPAGATION By cuttings in summer to early autumn. Not an easy plant for the home enthusiast without a heated propagator. Select strong firm pieces 10 cm long and remove the leaves from the lower half to two-thirds of each cutting. Insert the cutting into propagating mix, water thoroughly, and place a plastic bag over the top. A warm, shaded position indoors is suitable.
The cutting is weaned gradually prior to potting once the roots form.

environment. It is quite distinctive and has a more graceful habit than the species.

In common with other members of the fig family, the weeping fig has a small root system which is highly sensitive to cold, soggy soil. The drainage must be excellent. The growing mix should be airy and yet retain sufficient moisture to prevent rapid drying out.

Watering should be thorough and the soil allowed to dry slightly before watering again. This encourages strong root development. In cases of overwatering or underwatering, the foliage yellows and drops rapidly.

Ficus benjamina likes medium to brightly-lit conditions without direct sunlight; leaf chlorosis occurs if the light is too bright. Good humidity is essential in heated rooms and during the summer months. It is particularly sensitive to draughty conditions, so care should be taken when placing plants in the home.

Feeding is done on a regular basis with weak doses of fertilizer. Strong doses are not recommended and may cause damage to the roots and a loss of foliage.

115

The weeping fig prefers an even temperature, and growth can stagnate if this fluctuates widely. Unfortunately, plants sometimes suffer if moved from one position to another. They may lose foliage and stop growing for a few months until they adjust. Good humidity and particular diligence in watering is important at this time.

Ficus pumila & *F. radicans*   Creeping figs

B C F G H K   *

EASY CARE GUIDE

LIGHT Dull to well-lit; direct sunlight shining on the plant may burn or badly yellow the foliage.

TEMPERATURE 10° to 30°C, optimum 18°C. Growth may suffer in coldness and in hot, stuffy conditions.

WATERING Keep evenly moist, but not wet. Remove saucers from baskets in open ferneries during winter to prevent waterlogging.

FEEDING Spring to autumn. A small dose when dormant during the growing period is beneficial. Do not feed when dormant.

REPOTTING Early spring to mid-autumn, using a moist, well-drained, humus-rich potting mix. The root system is fine and small, so annual repotting is not generally needed. Ensure that plants awaiting repotting are moist. Disturb the roots as little as possible.

PESTS AND DISEASES Aphids, mite and mealy bug. Root rot.

Ficus pumila The small quilted leaves of this creeping fig are most attractive. The totem pole shows its natural habit to advantage.

Ficus radicans var. A slow growing creeper with thin wiry stems and attractive green and cream foliage. Keep it moist.

PROPAGATION Late summer to early spring by cuttings of semi-ripe shoots. Use only strong healthy pieces 5 to 8 cm long, from which the soft tips and the leaves from the bottom half of the cutting have been removed. Insert them into a moist mixture of three parts sand to one part peat, firm and water. Cover with a plastic bag and place in a warmish, light position. Inspect daily, water as needed and remove any dead leaves. Once rooted, gradually harden-off the cuttings before potting two to three into a 10 cm pot.

THE *FICUS* genus contains a surprising number of house plants whose hardiness in the cooler climates often belies their tropical origins. Besides the Indian rubber tree, *Ficus elastica* and the weeping fig, *Ficus benjamina*, there are the less commonly used creeping species, *F. pumila*, and *F. radicans variegata*.

Both species appreciate cool and airy conditions, but can withstand heating wherever there is sufficient humidity. In southern Australia they are suitable for inclusion in the fernery provided they receive no frosts.

F. pumila has small, round, medium-green leaves which are lightly quilted. In the spring the new growth is tinged an attractive light brown. It grows quickly once established and makes a superb totem pole or basket specimen. *F. radicans variegata* has a more compact habit, well suited to basket or pot culture. The spear-shaped foliage is a delightful combination of cream, green and grey.

117

The creeping figs develop tough and durable foliage in bright light. This tends to be softer in dull conditions. Both species have fine root systems which are sensitive to dryness or wetness. The soil should be kept evenly moist.

Totem pole specimens are easy to start. Place some well-established plants around the base of the pole and firm carefully. The pole should not wobble, yet the soil drainage should not be impeded. Train the young shoots around the pole so they overlap and cover it. Tie lightly with a flexible material.

Pruning of the tip produces a thicker, better-shaped plant. Hanging baskets in particular must be pruned to prevent thinning of the centre.

Gibasis   Tahitian bridal veil

B C F G H K   *

EASY CARE GUIDE

LIGHT Dull to well-lit; filtered light. Plants receiving too much light show a yellowing of the leaf accompanied by leaf-tip browning. Plants grown in poor light may not flower.

TEMPERATURE 10 to 30°C, optimum 18°C. Suitable for bush-houses and verandas in frost-free areas; an excellent greenhouse plant.

WATERING Moist at all times, drier in winter. Leaves yellow quickly and die if the plants dry out too much, and bud drop occurs. An ideal plant for hydroculture or self-watering pots.

HUMIDITY Generally unaffected by low levels, nonetheless plants soon lose their vigour and glossy lustre in hot, stuffy

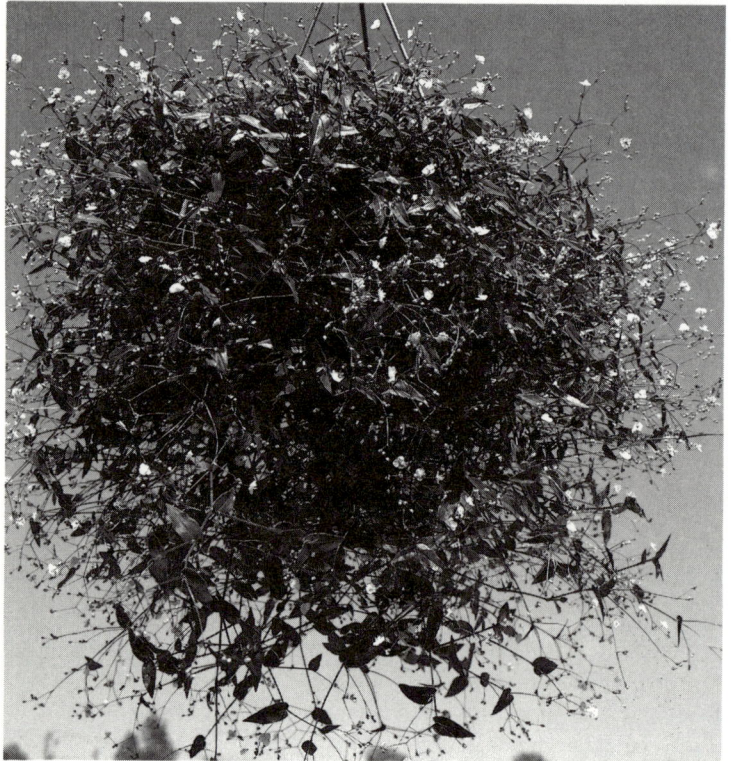

THE *GIBASIS* belongs to the same family as the *Tradescantia* (wandering Jew) which includes some colourful and exotic indoor and greenhouse plants, for example, *Dichorisandra, Setcreasea, Callisia, Rhoeo spathacea* (Moses in the cradle), and *Geogenanthus* (Seersucker plant).

Gibasis has shiny, attractive, olive green leaves with a purplish underside. As each shoot matures, a fine spray of greenish buds develops, finally opening in clusters of tiny, white, three-petalled flowers.

The Tahitian bridal veil is best grown where it can fully develop its naturally cascading habit. As a basket specimen it is a handsome addition to any home. Take care when handling plants because the thin stems break readily. Similarly guard against strong winds, in particular hot north winds. While the foliage is tough and withstands morning sun or filtered light all day, plants grown outdoors will burn or scorch if exposed to the hot afternoon summer sun.

Gibasis requires plenty of moisture during the warmer months. Baskets lined with coconut fibre and other porous materials need particular attention if grown outside. In hot and exposed outdoor positions plastic baskets are more practical. Take care that plants do not become waterlogged during the cooler months. In frost-prone parts of Australia, winter protection is essential.

For growth that is sturdy and compact, any well-lit aspect suffices. The bridal veil will grow in dull areas; however, it tends to grow leggy and flower less readily. Regular pinching and keeping it slightly on the dry side helps to overcome this tendency.

Make your own hanging basket using two to three sets of well-established plants in the centre of a 35 cm basket. Add potting mix, firm and water in. Allow at least half-a-thumb's depth between the mix and the basket lip for water.

atmospheres. Flowers may not open and leaf tips brown-off. Spray with room-temperature water as needed.

FEEDING Spring to autumn applications of an all-purpose plant food. Apply less in winter and in poorly-lit situations.

REPOTTING Throughout the year, using a moisture-retaining medium incorporating plenty of organic matter, for example peatmoss.

GENERAL CARE A thick, well-furnished plant is encouraged by regular trimming. Old plants must be pruned progressively or they may fail to respond.

PESTS AND DISEASES Aphid and mealy bug.

PROPAGATION As with many fast-growing plants, gibasis has a limited life span. New plants are easily started by taking numerous small pieces (5 cm) and putting them directly into tubes of potting mixture and covering them with a plastic bag. Root formation is rapid; pot-on as soon as established.

Maranta — Prayer plants

THE PRAYER plants (*Maranta*) are worthwhile including in a house plant collection for their lush velvety leaves, unusual flowers and general hardiness. They are known as prayer plants because they fold their leaves together at night-time. This should not be confused with the pro-

A C F H   ******

LIGHT Dull to well-lit. Avoid excessive bright light and heat. Suitable for artificial lighting. .

TEMPERATURE 7 to 25°C, optimal 15°C. Frost tender.

WATERING Moist but not wet during growing season; drier in winter. Use tepid water. Excessive dryness causes rapid yellowing and a general rolling of leaves.

HUMIDITY Regular misting of the leaves with room temperature water to prevent leaf-tip browning.

FEEDING Spring to early autumn, sparingly. Marantas burn if overfed — periodically flush out the soil with warm water.

REPOTTING Spring to early autumn using mixes of the African violet type to encourage strong root growth. Lighten heavy mixes with perlite. Use shallow pots.

PESTS AND DISEASES
Aphids, mealy bug and mite. Root rot.

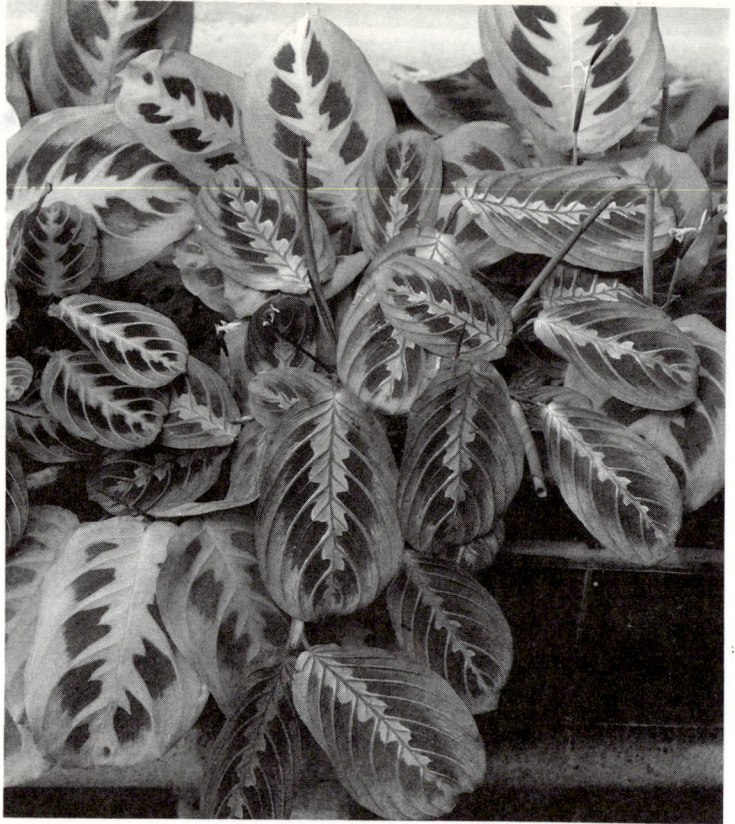

Maranta The ever-popular prayer plants are valued for terrariums.

tective response of rolling their leaves up during hot weather. This simple action 'reduces' the total surface of the leaf, thus lessening the heat stress and the requirement for water.

Three varieties of the species *M. leuconeura* are commonly grown. *M. l.* 'Kerchoveana' has pale-green leaves with chocolate blotches; *M. l.* 'Massangeana' has grey-green foliage blotched dark-green with whitish venation; and *M. l. erythroneura* (*M. tricolor*) is outstanding with dark-green foliage overlaid by light-green patches and red veins. It is commonly known as the red-veined prayer plant and bears lilac flowers. Other species include *M. bicolor* and *M.* 'Repens' (a trailer from England with smaller leaves similar to the ordinary prayer plant).

The maranta is at its best in the spring and early summer months. The old worn-out growth is replaced by vigorous new shoots emerging from below soil level. Encourage these by removing the old foliage as soon as the new shoots appear. They quickly develop into the large velvety leaves that are variously patterned.

Flowers appear throughout the year on thin, wiry stems. Spent flowering stems are best left to 'dry off' before attempting to remove them. If you wish to remove them before this, cut them off rather than pull them away — you will probably pull away large pieces of the plant as well.

Surprisingly, marantas are hardy plants even in cool situations. They do not like draughts and frosts, however, preferring warm, humid atmospheres. They blend in well among species grown under fluorescent lighting, e.g. *Saintpaulia*, where similar conditions prevail. The prayer plant has thin leaves which yellow and burn in very bright (or direct) sunlight. Best leaf colour and plant growth is achieved in medium light levels. They will grow successfully in dull areas but may tend to become straggly.

If you have had little success growing marantas in heated rooms, attention to humidity usually overcomes the problem. An unused aquarium or terrarium complete with light is a practical solution.

PROPAGATION Spring to autumn by cuttings and division.
Cuttings Select strong, healthy pieces of two to three leaves, cut below the node (leaf and stem joint) and dip the base in hormone powder. Pot into a three part sand to one part peat mixture, firm and water in. Cover with a plastic bag and stand in a warm, shaded position.
Division In spring, remove the plant from the pot and gently wash away the soil. Remove and discard all dead and worn out pieces. Select and pot the most vigorous young pieces. Treat as above until established.

Nephrolepis varieties

IN EVERY grouping of plants that enjoys widespread popularity, a number of 'sports' or mutations occur. The genus of the fishbone fern, *Nephrolepis*, is best known through one such — *N. exaltata* 'Bostoniensis', the superb boston fern (described next). It occurred as a sport in America, from which numerous other sports have evolved.

Undoubtedly the golden boston was a significant departure from the standard form, and has itself provided three distinct variations. There are two lacy varieties, 'Salome' and 'Chantilly Gold'; and an outstanding golden tassel named 'Delilah'. 'Delilah' is of particular merit, developing strong tasselled fronds which are quite upright when young and weep over the edge of the container as they mature.

The golden bostons require less water than the green varieties and at no stage will they tolerate prolonged overwatering. If anything, *slightly* dry is preferable, but

B C D E H K   ✱✱

EASY CARE GUIDE

LIGHT All varieties require plenty of filtered light. The scented fern tolerates dull positions; the gold varieties scorch in direct sun.
TEMPERATURE Bostons, 10 to 30°C; upright varieties, 15 to 30°C; scented varieties, 8 to 30°C.
WATERING Water all varieties thoroughly, allow to dry out slightly. Drier in winter. 'Florist Fancy' and 'Prince of Wales' dislike cold wet soil.

HUMIDITY All benefit from misting or standing the pots on constantly wet pebbles.

FEEDING Spring to autumn. Ferns respond to regular weak doses of the seaweed products, plus a slow-release fertilizer occasionally. Overfed plants are brittle and show little resistance to stress. Overfeeding takes months to correct.

REPOTTING Spring to autumn. If disturbed too much after active growth begins, some set-back may occur. The mix needs to be well-drained and rich in humus. Ferns do not need huge pots; advancement of one to two sizes is sufficient.

PROPAGATION Spring to autumn by division or spore.

Division Separate plantlets from the parent and pot or tube up. Do not pull them out of the pot; rather, remove the entire plant then gently cut out the plantlets. It is suggested that you discard heavily congested plants and start again using the young and more vigorous offsets.

Spore Spring. Fill a punnet with wet peatmoss. Sow the spore sparingly on the surface and place the punnet into an ice-cream container filled with 6 mm of water. Put the lid on the container, place in a warm position and keep the water level constant. Give the plants more light and harden-off before separating and potting-up.

Nephrolepis 'Prince of Wales' A striking fern suited only to indoor growing in a cool climate.

do not overdo this. To achieve the strong golden colour, plenty of bright filtered light is required. Unless some protection from the hot summer sun is provided, fronds will scorch and brown off. In less well-lit positions the fronds are an attractive lime-yellow colour.

Whereas the bostons have a spreading and weeping habit, there are occasions when space calls for upright and compact growth, as in a hallway or corner. Two unusual varieties that are suitable are the 'Prince of Wales' and 'Florist Fancy'. They come from a section of the genus *Nephrolepis* that is frost sensitive and must have warmer winter temperatures than the boston. If the temperature falls too low, they become dormant and may shed a lot of older growth. Both prefer well-lit positions avoiding direct sunlight, and only succeed in greenhouses or indoors in southern Australia. The unusual crinkled

Nephrolepis exaltata 'Delilah' *Grow the golden bostons in bright filtered light for strong colour and growth.*

Maranta *Prayer Plant Marantas are a low-light plant with beautiful foliage. They appreciate some warmth and humidity. Centre left Maranta l. 'Massangeana', centre right M.l. 'Erythroneura'.*

Gibasis *An unusual trailer with masses of white flowers atop deep green foliage. Prune it regularly to keep it compact.*

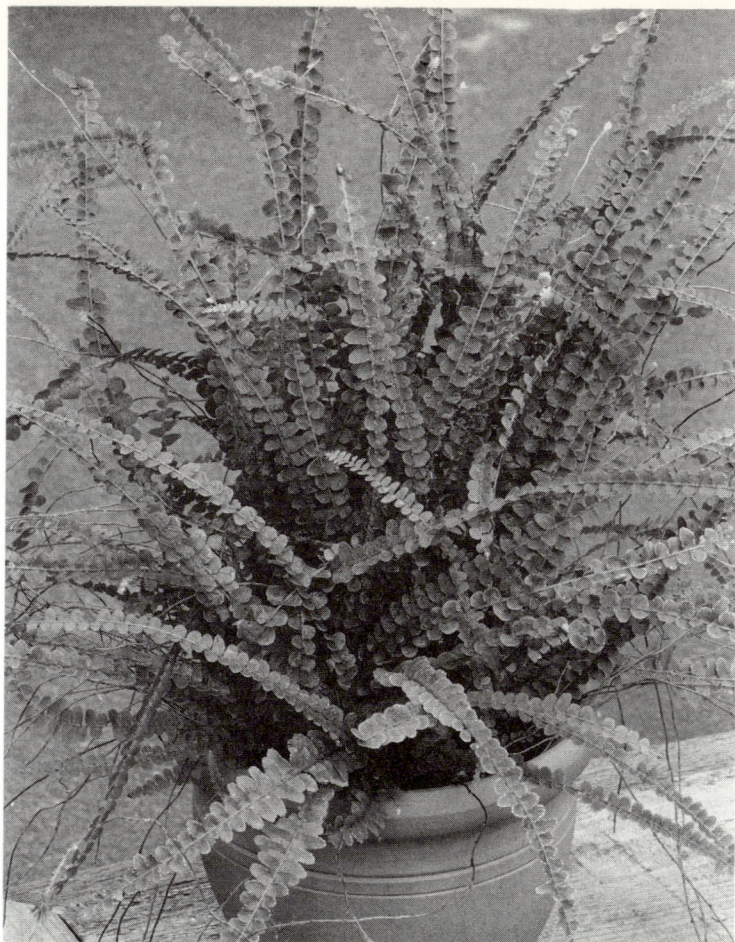

Nephrolepis cordifolia garrettii Tough compact growth and a mild perfume.

leaflets carried on stiff stems are a feature of these ferns, with the new growth covered by fine whitish hairs. 'Florist Fancy' is smaller with a tighter habit and distinctive upright growth, while the 'Prince of Wales' has elegant fronds that arch outwards as the plant develops.

The scented nephrolepis, *N. cordifolia garrettii*, belongs to the common fishbone group found in the home garden. It develops tuberous swellings on the roots which serve to store food and water for lean times. The idea of a scented lace appears bizarre, yet this one has a distinctive apricot or freesia perfume that is noticeable when the air is humid or the foliage is sprinkled with water. Each leaflet on the short fronds is rounded and deep green. It is a vigorous fern forming a thick clump in no time at all. This species is hardy for ferneries and well-protected outdoor areas, but will not withstand heavy frosts.

Nephrolepis exaltata 'Bostoniensis'   Boston fern

B C F G H K   *

FEW PLANTS rival the fern in popularity as a basket or for household decoration. Over the years the boston fern, *Nephrolepis exaltata* 'Bostoniensis', has established itself as suitable for continuous household culture. Its parent, *N. exaltata*, has an amazing distribution, occurring naturally in the tropical zones of Africa, Asia, Australia and South America. But although it is frost tender, it tolerates and thrives in quite chilly locations.

The boston fern responds well to light, producing broad, vigorous, light-green fronds in bright light. In dull areas the fronds are dark green. The finer forms, e.g. 'Smithii' and 'Verona', are more robust when grown with better light.

One problem for indoor fern growers is the drying out and browning of the leaflets. A lack of humidity is

Nephrolepis exaltata 'Bostoniensis' The graceful elegance of the hardy Boston fern is emphasized by an urn or hanging basket.

invariably the cause, although no amount of humidification counteracts the hot blast from a heating vent. Draughts, hot or cold, are to be avoided.

The boston fern is a moisture loving plant, but does not appreciate soggy wet soil. A thorough watering followed by a slight drying out is the best approach. In this way the fine root system must work hard and is more vigorous than in soggy soil.

Boston ferns are heavy feeders, although the finer forms ('Smithii' and 'Verona') produce sturdier fronds less prone to kinking or damage if they are kept slightly starved. Plants grown in porous baskets need more regular feeding to replace that leached by the extra water.

The boston fern is a low maintenance plant requiring an occasional thinning out of the old fronds. Any major renovation is done during repotting. It makes an excellent basket plant.

HUMIDITY Sit pots on saucers of pebbles which are kept wet. Mist foliage daily during hot dry spells.
FEEDING Spring to early autumn. Ferns become soft and weak if overfed, and less able to withstand adverse conditions. Both long-life and seaweed formulations are recommended. Do not feed dormant plants.
REPOTTING All year round. Repot into the next size container annually, using a well-drained mix with lots of humus. Cut away old and dead pieces of stems and roots. Place the crown at soil level.

GENERAL CARE The foliage responds to regular cleaning by gently showering with lukewarm water indoors. Beware of hosing plants outdoors in cold or sunny weather when they are susceptible to damage. The occasional yellow frond is no cause for alarm and merely indicates old age. Remove all tired fronds at the base.

PESTS AND DISEASES Scale, mealy bug and aphids. Scale are dotted *irregularly* over foliage and stems, and are not to be confused with the spore vessels which occur on the reverse side in *regular patterns*.
PROPAGATION By division or spore.
Division Late winter. Carefully remove all spent material, selecting the strong young crowns for repotting into small pots. Old crowns are discarded. Water sparingly until established.
Spore Spring. Fill a punnet with fine wet peatmoss or sieved potting mixture. Sow spore sparingly on the surface and place the punnet into an ice-cream container filled with 6 cm of water. Seal the container with the lid and set in a warm position. Adjust the water level. It may be necessary to cut some holes in the lid if the germinating spore stays too wet. At the 'kidney-shaped' stage gradually introduce the sporelings to more light and air before separating and potting-up into tubes.

Palms

THE PALM is a long-living house plant that adds a touch of elegance to the surroundings. There are a multitude of varieties with different habits of growth, together with varied and interesting leaf patterns. Not all species are suited to the colder climate, and some are best left to growers with heated greenhouses. Nonetheless, there are some excellent palms to choose from, such as the Rhapis (lady palm), *Arecastrum* (Cocos), *Howea* (kentia), *Chrysalidocarpus* (areca), *Phoenix* and *Chamaedorea*.

The kentia, *Howea*, was the parlour palm of Victorian

A B C F H K   *

EASY CARE GUIDE

LIGHT Dull to well-lit; tolerant of poor light. Avoid direct sunlight.
TEMPERATURE 7 to 30°C, optimal 15 to 20°C.
WATERING Keep moist, not wet; drier in winter.

FEEDING Regular weak doses of a balanced fertilizer. Do not feed during the winter resting period. Slow-release fertilizers are suitable.

REPOTTING All year. Palms are exceptionally tolerant of being pot-bound. If you choose a top quality mix with plenty of organic matter and good drainage, repotting once every 4 to 5 years is ample. Small plants are repotted regularly. Some thinning out of the roots is possible if great care is taken.

GENERAL CARE Regular cleaning of the foliage. Cut off dead fronds at the base and wait until the stump is completely dry before removing it.

PESTS AND DISEASES Aphids, scale, mealy bug and mite. Root rot.

PROPAGATION Palm seed germinates slowly and erratically. Follow the directions for each species. Suckers of the clustering types are carefully removed and potted-up.

Arecastrum *The Cocos plumosa palm is suitable for outdoor growing in frost-free areas. It also makes an excellent house plant.*

times. It is an outstanding specimen plant with its gently arching deep-green fronds. Some protection from frost in winter and the heat in summer is recommended for plants growing out of doors.

Another superb house palm is *Arecastrum roman-zoffianum* or the Cocos plumosa palm. It is fast growing and suitable only for rooms with high ceilings. It has soft feathery foliage which makes it a popular landscaping feature in protected gardens.

The dwarf parlour palm, *Chamaedorea elegans* (*Neanthe bella*), is a small, compact, slow-growing palm, valuable for homes with restricted space. Occasionally it bears sprays of small yellow flowers. It is seen to best advantage when a number of plants are clumped together.

The pigmy date palm, *Phoenix roebelinii*, is a favourite with first plant owners because it is hardy and easy to grow. A slow grower, it produces a feathery rosette of grey-green foliage from a stocky trunk. It is tolerant of warm or unheated conditions.

126

Chamaedorea elegans *For those requiring a slow-growing and compact palm, the dwarf parlour palm is suggested.*

One of the more striking palms is the strong-growing *Chrysalidocarpus lutescens*, the golden cane palm or areca. The stem of each frond is golden yellow which compliments the deep-green foliage perfectly. It also suckers and grows quickly. The golden cane palm has a spreading habit and takes up a lot of room.

The *Rhapis*, the lady palm, produces thickets of upright stems. The foliage is palm-shaped, deep-green and durable. It grows in ferneries or indoors and is of particular use in confined areas.

Some of the *Chamaedorea*, such as *C. erumpens*, bamboo palm, and *C. seifrizii*, reed palm, are multistemmed. They grow to around 3 m and have similar foliage to the dwarf parlour palm.

Palms prefer plenty of filtered light, good air circulation and humidity to prevent leaf-tips browning. Watering should keep the soil evenly moist but not saturated. During the cooler weather they may be kept slightly drier.

Peperomia

B D E H　　　******

EASY CARE GUIDE

LIGHT Dull to well lit; no
direct sunlight.
TEMPERATURE 15° to
25°C, optimum 15° to
18°C. Frost tender. Check
each type for special
requirements.
WATERING Use tepid
water; thoroughly moisten
the soil and then allow to
dry out slightly. The
'Emerald Ripples' types
resent excessive dryness
and will drop foliage. Keep
all varieties drier in winter.

THE *PEPEROMIA* is a member of the pepper family
to which the common black peppercorn, used as a
condiment, belongs. Peperomias are tropical plants. The
varieties commonly grown come from South America,
with other species native to Australia and New Guinea.'

The diversity in foliage, form and colour is quite amazing and at times deceptive. The leaves are generally quite
large and fleshy, with others small and thin. Their shape
— round, spoon-shaped or pointed — is often combined
with varying surface textures — velvety, smooth, hairy
or quilted. The peperomias form allows scope for the
different ways used to display plants, such as in hanging
baskets, in terrariums, and in mixed plantings.

P. caperata 'Emerald Ripples' is the best known of the
bushy species. Others in this group are *P. c.* 'Tricolor'; *P.
griseo-argentea* and varieties 'Blackie' and 'Pink Lady'; and

*Peperomia 'Emerald Ripples' One of the bushy varieties that grow best in
shallow containers.*

P. sandersii (watermelon peperomia). The best known trailer is *P. scandens* 'Variegata' with yellow and green foliage. It makes a superb basket specimen alone or in mixed plantings, responding very well to regular tip-pruning. Another trailer is *P. fosterii*. A third grouping incorporates bushy types with thick, fleshy stems and leaves, and a more open spreading habit. They are quite tolerant of dryness and stuffiness and perhaps are the hardiest of the genus. Included here are *P. obtusifolia* and *P. magnoliaefolia*.

A recent release is the beautiful *P.* 'Aussie Gold' with its brilliant coppery gold foliage and stems. It requires warmer temperatures than many species and should not be planted with other types.

Winter warmth and a dryish potting medium are important for peperomia culture in cool climates. They rot very quickly if they are kept cold and wet and are not suitable for ferneries. If your house is cold, keep the plants as dry as possible until the warmer weather returns. They may lose some older leaves, but soon recover.

Good light stimulates strong growth, but may bleach or burn the foliage if it is too bright.

HUMIDITY Sit plants on a saucer of wet pebbles; the pot must not sit in the water. Excessive humidity in a terrarium may cause rotting. Improve ventilation as necessary.

FEEDING Spring to autumn using half normal strength. Overfed peperomias become brittle, soft and sappy and may collapse totally. Do not feed during winter in cold or poorly lit rooms.

REPOTTING A light, airy mixture suitable for African violets ensures a strong root system. Normally repotting once every 18 to 24 months suffices. Use wide, shallow containers.

GENERAL CARE Shower lightly with tepid water to remove dust. Remove spent flowers and foliage.

PESTS AND DISEASES Aphids. Crown and root rot. Botrytis.

PROPAGATION Spring to autumn by stem cuttings, leaf cuttings and seeds. *Stem cuttings* Cut a strong healthy piece of stem into sections of three to four leaves with a sharp knife. Remove the bottom half of the foliage and insert the cutting into a one part peat to one part perlite mixture. Firm and water well. *Leaf cuttings* With a sharp knife select a leaf from the middle of the plant. Shorten the stem to 3 cm and gently plant it to half its length in the mixture above. A temperature of 15° to 20°C is required. *Seeds* These form on the unusual flower spikes and are sown on the surface of the mixture above. Once germinated, feed regularly until large enough to be transplanted into tubes.

Philodendron cordatum

A TROPICAL, yet hardy, species adapted to cool growing is the well-known *Philodendron cordatum*. It is one of the range of climbing philodendrons which is grown in Victoria and other cool-winter climates as an indoor plant.

This philodendron is one of the best and most durable house plants. It seems indifferent to hardship, and grows satisfactorily in conditions where others fail. Poor light, erratic watering and stuffiness are three difficulties this

B C F H   *

EASY CARE GUIDE

LIGHT Dull to well lit. Excess light causes blotching and yellowing. Growth in dull light is weaker and slower.

TEMPERATURE 8° to 30°C, optimum 12° to 20°C.

WATERING Keep moist, but drier in winter. Philodendrons dislike wet feet, preferring to dry out slightly between waterings. This promotes healthy root growth. Use tepid water.

FEEDING Regular feeding with half-strength fertilizer ensures strong, sturdy plants. Should growth become soft and weak, adjust strength and frequency.

REPOTTING Spring to early autumn. Annual repotting is not necessary although topping-up with fresh soil is beneficial. This philodendron will grow to a large size in a small container, but if it is too pot-bound growth is retarded. Use well-aerated mixtures rich in humus.

PESTS AND DISEASES Scale, aphids and mealy bug. Root rot.

PROPAGATION Cuttings in spring to early autumn. Tip cuttings with two to three leaves are taken from the parent plant and inserted immediately into moist sphagnum moss or a standard cutting mixture. Firm and water well. Cover with a plastic bag, and place in a warmish spot with moderate light. Inspect regularly for pests and disease. Node or bud cuttings are prepared by cutting just above the leaf and bud, and 2.5 cm below. If cuttings are thin, use multiple nodes. Treat as above, and pot into small pots once established.

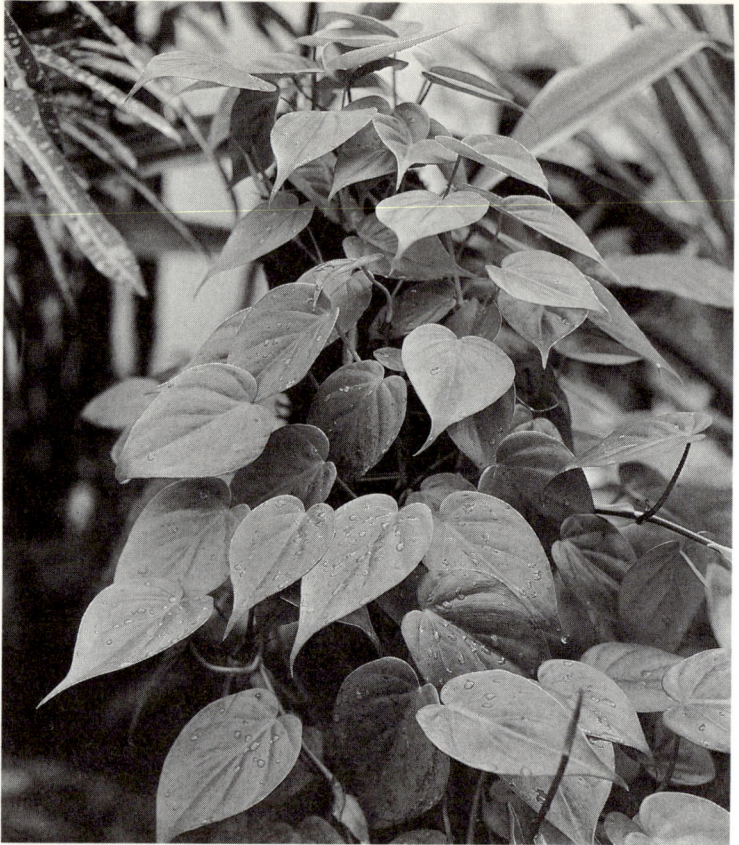

Philodendron cordatum *A long-standing favourite with newcomers to house plants. Hardy, adaptable and versatile.*

plant tolerates. The foliage is heart–shaped, olive green and tinged with copper when young.

Two other forms are *Philodendron cordatum variegatum*, lightly-veined with cream; and the newer *P. c.* 'Golden Pride'. 'Golden Pride' is slower growing with foliage that is a golden–yellow in bright light and lime coloured in less well-lit situations.

The leaves are produced on a vigorous vine which attaches itself to any convenient surface by aerial roots. This climbing habit lends itself to training the plant across doorways, ceilings and dividing screens, and in hanging baskets or up a totem pole. To encourage these roots to adhere securely, tie the new shoots firmly, but not tightly, against the pole. Tying restricts sideways movement while encouraging upward growth.

If planting your own totem pole, use a pole of the full height you require because repotting of an established plant is difficult. Should your plant need repotting and it is impossible to move it, remove the old pot and sit the root ball inside a larger pot. Fill the space with fresh potting soil (do *not* sit the plant any deeper). The roots will find their way into the new soil, thus avoiding disturbance and damage.

For the busy gardener, *Philodendron cordatum* is second to none. It requires little maintenance, except for occasional dusting, feeding and watering.

Schefflera arboricola Dwarf umbrella tree

B D F H ******

EASY CARE GUIDE

LIGHT Dull to well-lit. Avoid direct sunlight as foliage burns or yellows. Turn regularly to maintain even development.

TEMPERATURE 15 to 30°C, optimum 15°C. The dwarf umbrella is suitable for the bush-house and veranda, but protection from frost and cold wind is essential in winter.

WATERING Keep moist, not wet; drier in winter. Allow to dry out slightly between waterings. This encourages sturdiness and a strong root system. Early leaf drop occurs from underwatering.

HUMIDITY Surprisingly tolerant of air-dryness yet appreciative of humidity. Spray leaves twice weekly and sit on a saucer of moist pebbles.

FEEDING Spring to early autumn, with slow-release or seaweed formulations. Never force plants during their resting periods, or in poorly-lit areas.

Schefflera arboricola A hardy selection of umbrella tree with masses of palm-like leaves and a compact habit.

131

Aphids, scale, mealy bug and mite.
PROPAGATION By seeds or air layering.
Seeds Summer and spring. Sow onto seed compost, cover lightly with mix and place a sheet of glass over the top. A temperature of 22 to 25°C ensures rapid germination. Harden-off gradually before potting into tubes either singly or in multiples.
Air layers Spring and summer. Carefully remove leaves from a 15 cm section of stem and wrap it in a wad of moist sphagnum moss. Enclose thoroughly with plastic and tie firmly top, bottom and middle to retain the moisture, add extra water as required during root formation. Once the new roots are in ample evidence, carefully sever the new plant, remove plastic and pot up with the sphagnum intact. Water thoroughly and place in a warm, dull position. Move into more light as the plant acclimatizes.

THE DWARF umbrella tree, *Schefflera arboricola*, is another of the recent introductions of house plants that has been an outstanding success. The glossy foliage stands out from the stems and is close enough together to give a bushy effect. Each leaf is comprised of a number of fresh green leaflets arranged around the leaf stem.

There are several varieties available. 'Renate' has each leaflet interestingly cut; and there is a gold variegated form. Both are as hardy as the species and require the same culture.

The reason for the appeal of the dwarf umbrella tree lies in the ease of culture. This species is less sensitive to overwatering and drying out, but nonetheless prefers an evenly moist potting mix. It is accommodating of cooler weather and less inclined to drop foliage when temperature changes are sudden.

Plenty of bright, filtered light is preferred for strong growth, although it will grow satisfactorily in low-light areas.

Pruning of the dwarf umbrella tree is straightforward and helps produce a superior plant by encouraging development of side shoots. Whenever you prune, make it a rule never to cut back to old leafless wood. Some healthy foliage must be retained, and any programme of rejuvenation is best done progressively to lessen the shock. Potting calls for a well-drained mixture with plenty of organic matter. The root system is vigorous, but will live in a small container provided it has adequate feeding.

Stenochlaena palustris   Queensland climbing fern

B C F H K   ✱✱

EASY CARE GUIDE

LIGHT Dull to well-lit; no direct sunlight.
TEMPERATURE 10 to 20°C, optimum 18°C. For higher temperatures increase the humidity. Frost tender. Suited for bush-houses in warmer areas.

MANY OF the plants now regarded as commonplace were previously limited to the collector. They were difficult to propagate and expensive. The Queensland climbing or swamp fern, *Stenochlaena palustris*, is one which can now be obtained readily through the use of tissue culture.

It is an epiphyte with vigorous fleshy stems and aerial roots that adhere to the moist bark of the host. These stems are reddish brown and covered with similarly toned scales.

The foliage is a light shiny green, serrated at the edges

Stenochlaena A young tissue-cultured plant with multiple stems. A vigorous fern requiring a large basket.

WATERING Keep moist at all times. It is a very thirsty fern in hot weather; the self-watering pot is recommended.

HUMIDITY AND AIR Keep the air humid in still, stuffy environments where temperatures exceed 25°C. Some fresh air is advantageous, but avoid draughts.

FEEDING Spring to late summer. Do not feed during winter dormancy.

REPOTTING Anytime with a good water-retaining mix full of organic matter.

PESTS AND DISEASES Aphids, scale and mealy bug.

GENERAL CARE Cut off old fronds and prune the stems to give a bushier plant.

PROPAGATION By spore or stem cuttings.

Spore Spring. Sow the spore sparingly onto a fine moist medium. Sit the tray in an ice-cream container with 6 cm of water in the bottom, and seal. Place in a warm spot out of the sun, ventilate occasionally. As the sporelings develop, wean gradually. Pot into tubes when large enough to handle.

Stem cuttings Spring to autumn. Cut the stems into 10 to 15 cm sections. Pot them to half their length in propagating mix. Locate in a warm, well-lit position. Move into potting soil once established.

and tough. The young growth at certain times of the year is a burnished bronze, darkening as it matures. In dull conditions the older leaves are a dark green. These leaves are the sterile fronds and fortunately outnumber the less-attractive fertile or spore bearing fronds. Quite a number of ferns display this habit of bearing separate reproductive fronds, including *Lygodium* and *Blechnum*. These fertile fronds are narrow and filamentous, forming a tangled mass and bearing brown spores along their length.

Plants are raised from spore in the usual manner — ensure the sowing surface remains moist at all times. The other method of propagation is by cuttings of the stems. This may not always be an easy task as those adhering to a slab tear if handled roughly. It is important to plant

133

them the right way up — sometimes it is safer to lay them on their sides and cover with the mixture.

The value of tissue culture now becomes apparent. Large stocks of parent material for cuttings or spore production are no longer necessary. The young tissue cultures are grown as clumps, thus producing better-quality plants with multiple stems. Stenochlaena is a rapid grower that needs a constant supply of moisture. The self-watering pots and baskets with a reservoir of water at the base are ideal.

It is a frost-tender plant, but will grow in a fernery provided it is protected adequately. A badly frost-affected plant seldom recovers.

It grows well either as a pot or basket plant. The main consideration is plenty of room for the vigorous and rambling stems to grow over. Baskets in particular can be a size or two larger than normal because repotting an established plant is difficult without losing some stems. The fibre-lined basket is better looking than the plastic basket, but impossible to repot once the stems work through the fibre.

You can thicken up an old plant by cutting back the stems progressively over the warmer months.

Syngonium 'White Butterfly'

THE TROPICAL family *Araceae* is the source of many useful and decorative house plants. One genus of the family that has come to the forefront is *Syngonium*, especially following the introduction of the versatile variety 'White Butterfly' that continues to be one of the toughest and best house plants, and is recommended to the novice indoor gardener.

The syngoniums withstand exceptionally low light levels, periods of dryness and being pot-bound. Under poor light, growth slows right down, consequently water and fertilizer requirements are greatly reduced. In fact a little dryness helps to keep plants compact, but may cause early leaf death if carried to extremes.

An interesting feature of 'White Butterfly' is the differences in leaf shapes as the plant grows. Young foliage is quite round, while older leaves take on the unusual

Syngonium 'White Butterfly' *Few plants surpass* 'White Butterfly' *for versatility and hardiness. Tolerant of low light, it has attractive creamy yellow and green foliage.*

FEEDING Spring to autumn. A little often for sturdy growth. Do not feed over the winter if growth ceases.

HUMIDITY In hot stuffy conditions, marginal leaf browning may occur. Mist foliage or sit pots on saucers of wet pebbles.

REPOTTING 'White Butterfly' has a small vigorous root system. Yearly repotting is unnecessary; top up with fresh soil. Use well-aerated and humus-rich mixes.

GENERAL CARE A little shower with tepid water monthly to remove dust. Remove dead leaves. Prune back leggy growth.

PESTS AND DISEASES Scale, aphids, mite and mealy bug. Root rot.

PROPAGATION By cuttings from spring to autumn. *Cuttings* Tip or node cuttings with two to three leaves are stuck directly into a standard propagating mix. Firm, water well. Cover with a plastic bag, place in a warmish spot with filtered light.

arrowhead shape. The fresh lemony-lime tonings are attractive and fit into most colour schemes.

Other worthwhile varieties include *S. auritum* 'Fantasy' with green and white marbling; *S. podophyllum* 'Green and Gold', *S.* 'Noak' and *S. albo-lineatum* which are green and cream combinations; and two dark-pink forms, *S.* 'Pinkie' and *S.* 'Maya Red'.

'White Butterfly' is propagated by the modern method of tissue culture. This maintains the bushy habit which makes the 'White Butterfly' so popular. Cutting-grown plants tend to be less bushy. Judicious pruning of the trailers promotes plenty of side shoots and a thicker plant.

The trailing or climbing habit gives extra ways to grow the plant. 'White Butterfly' is a superb hanging basket specimen, needing only average household conditions, and makes an excellent totem pole.

135

To quickly cover a totem pole, plant three uniform plants in a well-draining mix.

Growing a hanging basket is simple and straight-forward. Plant two to three small bushy plants in the centre of the basket using a well-drained potting mixture. From then on water and feed as necessary. Keep an eye out for insect pests.

The totem pole is an attractive idea for narrow areas where space is at a premium or where height is preferred. Select a good-sized pot, say a 20 to 25 cm pot, and a sturdy piece of bark, large enough for future growth. Secure the bark in place with potting mix and firm light-ly. Arrange two to three plants around the totem pole, nestling them close enough for the roots to cling. Use a flexible material such as wool or nylon ribbon to lightly, but firmly, tie the growing shoots against the bark. These are removed once the aerial roots have securely adhered to the support. Wire ties strangle expanding stems and should not be used.

Syngoniums are very successful as hydroculture subjects.

Tolmeia menziesii   Piggy-back plant

THE PIGGY-BACK plant, *Tolmeia menziesii*, is one of those evergreen hardy plants that serve well for interior decoration. The pleasantly green foliage is both bold and soft, gently cascading over the pot or basket lip. It is tolerant of the cold and suited to ferneries, greenhouses (heated or cold) and verandas. Beware of frosts however and, at the opposite extreme, the scalding winds of summer. Tolmeias prefer coolness to heat, and indeed rarely survive in hot airless conditions.

The standard variety, *T. menziesii*, has a delightful fresh green lobed leaf covered with whitish hairs. The leaves develop plantlets at their base as they mature and it is from this habit that their name of piggy-back derives. The leaves, together with their plantlets, are used for propagation and root readily if placed in water or propagating mixture. It is recommended that this is done regularly as piggy-back plants tend to be short-lived and may die all at once for no apparent reason.

Tolmeia A good choice for the cold home, the piggy-back prefers filtered light and even moisture.

A C F G H K   *

EASY CARE GUIDE

LIGHT Medium filtered light; no direct sun.
TEMPERATURE 7°C to 25°C, optimum 15°C to 18°C.
WATERING Keep moist at all times, drier in winter. Keep water clear of the crown. Thorough watering in hot weather is essential. Continually drooping foliage may indicate root collapse; in this case extra water only exacerbates the problem and affected plants are best discarded.

HUMIDITY In heated rooms and during hot dry spells, mist regularly and sit the pot on a saucer of wet pebbles. Red spider is deterred by high humidity.

AIR Fresh air is essential in hot weather, particularly indoors. Avoid draughts and hot drying winds.

FEEDING Tolmeias will utilize as much food as is supplied, but not always to advantage. High nitrogen formulations give plenty of lush growth which may not, however, have much substance or strength to withstand hardship, for example a missed watering. Feed 'a little, often', and cease when the plant becomes dormant.

REPOTTING Any time, using a well-draining, humus-rich potting mixture. Disturb the root system as little as possible and move into a container two sizes bigger. Tolmeias have a fine spreading root system and prefer squat pots.

PESTS AND DISEASES Mealy bug and mite. Root and crown rot.

PROPAGATION Under no circumstances attempt to divide a piggy-back plant. The crowns are tightly packed and will not separate without a lot of damage. Leaf propagation is the easiest and best method. Select a strong, healthy leaf which has a well-developed plantlet at its base. Shorten the leaf stalk to approximately 3 to 4 cm and insert this into a three part sand to two part peat mix up to the base of the leaf. Very big leaves are best trimmed. Roots quickly emerge from the base of the leaf. Place a plastic bag over the cutting after watering. A warm, well-lit position aids root production. Pot up as soon as struck into small pots.

A recent addition is the golden speckle piggy-back, a delightfully variegated form liberally splashed with golden yellow. It has the same cultural needs as the green form, although a little more light is needed for best colour. It can be propagated similarly.

Tolmeias grow best in a cool, well-lit situation both indoors and out. If light levels are too bright, leaf yellowing and stunting may occur, while in very dull aspects growth is weak and spindly.

Plants situated in hot, stuffy rooms invariably become dull in appearance and develop brown edges on the leaves. Mite thrives in such atmospheres and will very quickly destroy a healthy plant. Foliage attacked by mite shows a slight puckering accompanied by an unusual yellowing. As the pest entrenches itself a fine webbing appears on the underside of the leaves and in severe cases envelops the plant. Do not hesitate to destroy such plants immediately and spray nearby specimens (except ferns) with a miticide.

Rapid growth is a feature of the piggy-back plant, thus lending it to basket culture. The naturally cascading habit ensures that not too much of the basket is visible; and makes it an especially attractive specimen plant for table decoration. Occasionally the pale green and red flowers on slender stems appear, but usually only on cold-grown plants.

Good moisture levels are required, bearing in mind that overwatering and poor drainage during the cooler seasons causes crown and root rot. During these periods keep them slightly drier and remove the saucers from any plastic baskets outdoors to ensure rapid drainage of water.

Phoenix roebelinii *A slow grower, the pigmy date palm is an attractive specimen plant.*

Syngonium auritum 'Fantasy' A hardy variety of the goosefoot family. A delightful mixture of white and deep green foliage.

BELOW Aspidistra The toughest of all house plants, growing in exceptionally dull conditions when required.

Brief
Descriptions

Acorus gramineus

A delightful, low-growing plant with narrow, glossy green and gold foliage. It prefers a cool to warm position with filtered light. Keep evenly moist. Ideal for terrarium culture. Easily propagated by division.

A C F H   *

Acorus *A slow growing plant that is well suited for use in a terrarium.*

Adiantum capillus-veneris   Maidenhair fern

A C F G H K   *   A low, clumping maidenhair fern suited to cool conditions. A hardy species. Keep evenly moist. Suitable for use in terrariums. Slugs and snails may be a problem. Propagation is by division of the creeping rhizome and spores.

Adiantum capillus-veneris A hardy, cool-growing maidenhair for an unheated greenhouse or fernery.

Adiantum hispidulum   Rough maidenhair

A B C F G H K   *   *Adiantum hispidulum This variety may be grown successfully in the fernery. It is cold-hardy, but protect from frosts.*

A hardy species with unusually tough fronds well suited to outdoor and fernery cultivation. Tolerant of poor to well-lit conditions but not hot winds. Keep evenly moist. A low-growing fern useful in terrariums. Watch for slugs and snails. Propagation is by spore.

Ardisia Coral berry plant

The coral berry is a small, eye-catching shrub with bright-red (or white) berries and star-shaped flowers. The deep-green leaves are lightly scalloped and glossy. A tough, cold grower for fernery, porch, cool greenhouse and indoor use. Scale may attack them. Propagation is by seed or cutting.

B C F G H K   *

Ardisia The red berries contrast effectively with the white flowers and glossy deep green foliage.

Asparagus Asparagus fern

The delicate ferny foliage of the asparagus makes them worth including in any house plant selection. They are exceptionally hardy and tolerate the heat and cold. They prefer some humidity, and a moist potting soil. *A. densiflorus* and *A. d.* 'Myer's' are superb basket plants. They grow easily from seed.

B C F G H K   *

See colour plates.

Aspidistra Cast iron plant

A C F G H K   *   The aspidistra is aptly named the cast iron plant. It will grow in the dullest and coldest of positions. It has small, purplish, star-shaped flowers. The long tapering leaves are deep-green and durable. *A. elatior variegata* is attractively striped gold and cream. Propagation is by division in early spring.
See colour plates.

Begonia 'Cleopatra'

B D E G H   **   An attractive begonia with green-yellow and brown foliage, and scented pinkish flowers. A rhizomatous variety. Avoid direct sunlight. Reduce watering during the cooler months. Ideal for basket or terrarium culture. Mildew can be a problem. It is propagated by leaf cutting, stem cutting or division.

Begonia Cleopatra *The beautifully marked foliage of this begonia is of particular merit. The lightly scented pink flowers are a bonus.*

Begonia rex Rex begonia

B D E G H   **   The rex begonia is grown for the spectacularly coloured foliage of many shades and patterns. Good light develops the colour, but avoid direct sunlight. A light, airy and

Begonia rex *The striking markings of the rex begonia make them a valuable foliage house plant.*

moist potting mixture is suitable. In cold temperatures it becomes dormant and should be kept drier. The flowers are best removed. Mildew can be troublesome. Propagation is by seed or leaf cutting.

Brassaia — Umbrella tree

B D E H   ✳✳

Brassaia actinophylla *The umbrella tree with its bold foliage prefers a well-lit situation.*

The umbrella tree is still a popular house plant with glossy, medium-green foliage divided into segments. At no stage must the soil become saturated. A well-drained potting mix is suggested. They prefer to be slightly pot-bound. Avoid draughts. Mite, scale and aphids are potential pests. Propagation is by air layering old plants or by seeds.

Caladium

B D F H   ***   The unusual and colourful foliage of these tuberous plants is always admired. They need bright, filtered light and warm, moist soil for success. Withhold all water once the foliage begins to yellow and store the tuber in dry peat. Restart them in a moist sand and peatmoss mix in early summer. Watch for mite and aphids. Propagation is by seed or dividing older tubers.

Caladium *The caladium is a tuberous plant with richly patterned leaves. It needs warmth for best results.*

Ceropegia woodii   Chain of hearts

B C E H   *   The rosary vine or chain of hearts, *Ceropegia woodii*, is the best known member of the trailing ceropegias. A hardy pot plant which prefers being pot-bound and slightly dry. The small, round leaves are in pairs and are grey-

Ceropegia woodii The chain of hearts with its long trailers is best grown in a basket. It has unusual lantern-shaped flowers.

green. Small, upright, lantern-shaped flowers are produced throughout the year. Propagation is by seed, cutting or by the aerial 'tubers' which develop along the stems. Bury the 'tuber' to half its depth in washed river sand and keep just moist until new growth begins.

Chlorophytum   Spider plant

Chlorophytum A versatile plant, the spider plant is equally at home indoors, on the porch or in a fernery.

A B C F G H K   ✻

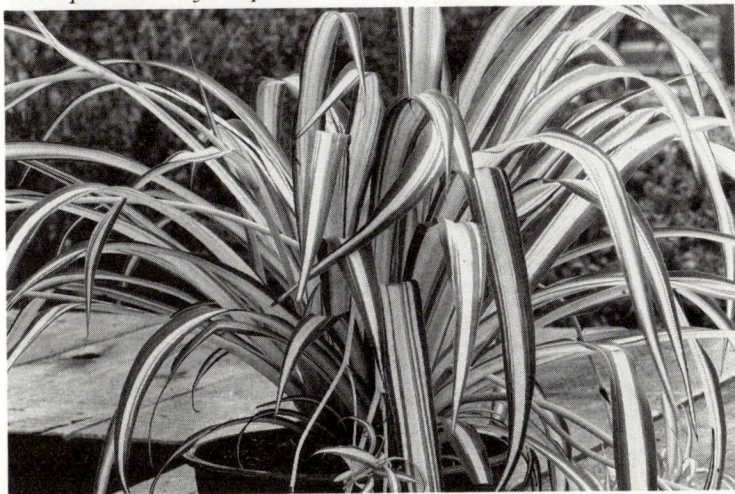

The spider plant is hard to beat as an all-purpose house plant. It is hardy and easy to grow. The shiny foliage is arranged in a rosette, from which long flower stalks grow and develop plantlets at their tips. The variegated varieties are suitable for pot or basket, but keep them away from strong wind. Aphids can be a problem. Propagation is from the plantlets.

Coleus

B C F G H J K   *   The bright, multi-coloured foliage of the *Coleus* is always appealing. A fast-growing annual for summer and autumn decoration. They are very thirsty and need regular weak applications of fertilizer. Pinch back for bushier plants, and remove all flowers. Grow from seed or cutting.

Coleus Coleus are easy to grow from seed. They come in many colours and leaf shapes.

Cordyline

B D F H   **   The Cordyline is closely related to the Dracaena and requires similar conditions. Broad leathery foliage in the red, pink, brown and yellow tonings. Keep moist, drier in winter. Mist regularly in hot, dry atmospheres. Mite can be a problem. Propagation is by air layers, cuttings or seed.

Cordyline *A decorative group of broad-leaved house plants with contrasting foliage.*

Fatsia Aralia

An ideal plant for low-light areas including the fernery and veranda. The large, palm-shaped leaves are most attractive. Cold-grown plants produce heads of greenish flowers and indigo berries. Provide extra humidity for plants in heated rooms. Watch out for mite, scale and aphids. Easy and quick to grow from seed.

A C F G H K   ✳

Fatsia *Thrives in a cool position indoors or out.*

Fittonia

A D F H   ******

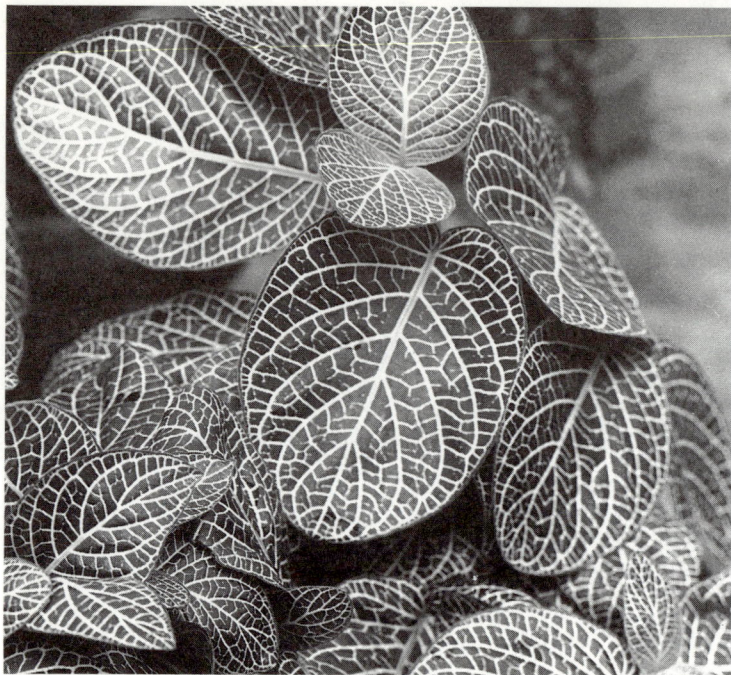

Fittonia *Recommended for terrarium culture. They thrive in warm humid conditions with filtered light.*

The low-growing nerve plants are perfect for terrarium culture. They need high humidity and brown-off in hot stuffy atmospheres. The best known are *F. verschaffeltii argyroneura* with a soft-green leaf veined ivory, and its miniature form 'Silver Pixie'. Pink and red forms are also grown. Pinch back leggy growth, and do not overfeed. They resent cold, wet soil and low temperatures. Propagation is by cutting.

Gynura

B D F H   ******   Purple is an uncommon colour for foliage house plants and always causes comment. The velvet plant is a vigorous trailer for baskets with a bright, velvety-purple leaf. It needs bright light for best colour. Pinch regularly and remove the orange flowers. Aphids are attracted to this plant. Propagation is by cutting.

Gynura *A vigorous rambler that benefits from regular tip pruning. Attractive purple foliage and orange flowers.*

Hedera

The ivy is one of the earliest and best house plants. It is hardy, adaptable and straightforward to grow in pots and baskets. The many varieties include small, compact types and large vigorous growers. Leaf colour is green or variegated. They dislike hot, stuffy conditions and prefer cool, airy situations. Pinch back regularly. Feed only during the spring to autumn period. Mites, scale and grubs are the major pests. They are easily propagated from cuttings.

A B C F G H J K ∗

Hedera *The ivy remains one of the best all-purpose house plants, being easy to grow and tolerant of cold temperatures.*

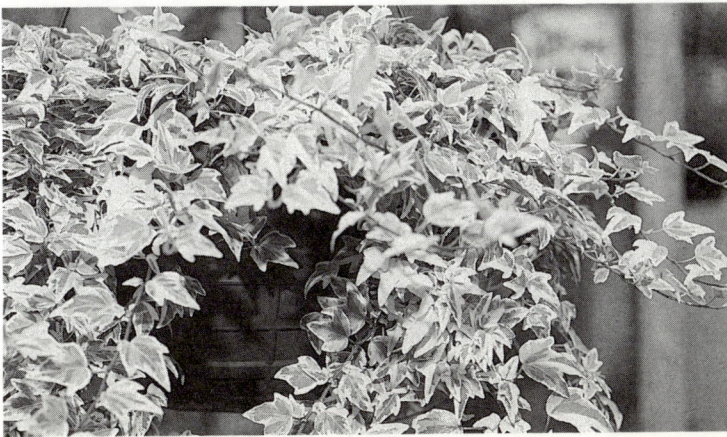

149

Helxine soleirolii   Baby's tears

A C F G H K   ✱   Baby's tears is one of the easiest of plants to grow. A fast-growing small leaved creeper useful for terrariums, covering rocks in ferneries and baskets. Outdoors a haven for slugs and snails. Do not feed excessively. Moist at all times. Simple to propagate from cuttings.

Helxine 'Baby's Tears' *A delightful, close-growing ground cover that makes a superb basket.*

Lamium galeobdolon   Aluminium creeper

A B C F G J K   ✱   *Lamium The attractively scalloped foliage splashed with silver makes the aluminium creeper a valuable foliage plant.*

150

A versatile fast-growing creeper with soft green and silver foliage, and yellow flowers. Well suited to pot or basket culture, and as ground cover in ferneries. Prune regularly. It is easily grown by cutting.

Microcoelum weddeliana Baby cocos palm

B D F H   **★★**

A dainty and highly decorative indoor palm for well-lit areas with no direct light. Keep moist, but not wet. The fronds are dark green with a silver edging. Slow growing — can be used in terrariums. Mite is sometimes a problem. Seed is the method of propagation.

Microcoelum weddeliana An elegant palm with finely cut fronds and an attractive trunk.

Monstera deliciosa
Fruit salad plant

B C E G H K   *   The hardy *Monstera* has tough, leathery rounded leaves which are deeply cut and holed in the manner of Swiss cheese. An adaptable plant which grows indoors, and outdoors in a protected fernery. The fruit is soft and tastes like fruit salad. An outstanding specimen plant. Propagation is by seed or stem cutting.

Monstera *The durable monstera with its large, deeply cut leaves is a first-class house plant.*

Oplismenus
Rainbow grass

B C F G H   *   Rainbow grass is a rapid growing trailer which makes a superb basket. Small pointed leaves, green in colour and edged pinkish-white. Reddish flowers. Trim regularly and protect from frost. It is readily propagated by cuttings.

152

Oplismenus *This quick growing grass looks its best in a basket. Regular trimming keeps it bushy.*

Pilea

Pileas are small bushy house plants noted for their attractive leaves. The aluminium plant, *P. cadierei*, is best known for the beautiful silver and green of its foliage. *P. mollis* 'Moon Valley' has quilted lime-green and chocolate leaves; *P. microphylla*, the military fern, has small green foliage; and *P. nummulariaefolia* 'Creeping Charlie' is a fresh green. All need winter warmth and a moist, airy mix. The smaller varieties are useful in terrariums. Prune regularly. Propagation is simple using cuttings and seeds.

B D E H   ******

Pilea cadierei 'minima' A dwarf form of the popular aluminium plant for unheated greenhouses or indoor growing.

Plectranthus Swedish ivy

A B C F G H K ***** Adaptable foliage house plants for pot or basket growing. Tolerant of dull to well-lit conditions. Prune regu-
larly. Three types of note: *P. nummularis* with fresh green
leaves and spreading habit; *P. nummularis variegata*, the
cream and green form; and *P. oertendahlii*, a soft leaved
variety grey-green in colour, veined white. Easy to
propagate by cuttings.

*Plectranthus Fast growing ramblers for the fernery, porch or inside.
Attractive fresh foliage.*

Pteris Brake ferns

A C F G H J K ****** The brake fern family contains many hardy varieties for
the fernery, cool greenhouse and indoors. A cool, airy
and well-lit aspect is desirable. They must not dry out.
Some species need more warmth. Slugs, snails and
aphids attack them. Propagation is by spore.

Asparagus *Good stand-by houseplants tolerant of most conditions. Keep them moist.*

Senecio rowleyanus *The string of beads is a trailing succulent which requires bright light. Keep it dryish.*

Pteris The Brake ferns are an interesting group well suited to cool growing. They blend well in fernery plantings.

Sansevieria Snake plant

Sansevieria The golden snake plant is an excellent choice for hot, brightly lit rooms. An exceptionally tough plant.

A B C E H P   ✳

155

There are many varieties of the tough snake plant. There are low growers such as *S. parva* and *S. trifasciata* 'Hahnii', the impressive tall growing *S. liberica*, and the popular green and gold *S. trifasciata* 'Laurentii'. They tolerate moist conditions indoors, both cool to hot and dull to well–lit. They use little water and rot if kept wet. Over winter keep them dryish. The flowers are greenish and sweetly perfumed. Propagation is by division, seeds or leaf cuttings (green varieties only).

Saxifraga stolonifera   Strawberry begonia

B C E G H   *   The small round leaves and trailing habit of this Saxifraga are most attractive. The leaf is grey-green with white veins. A variegated form, *S. stolonifera* 'Tricolor', has broad creamy-white margins tinged pink. Unusual white flowers. Keep pot-bound. They propagate easily by the young plantlets.

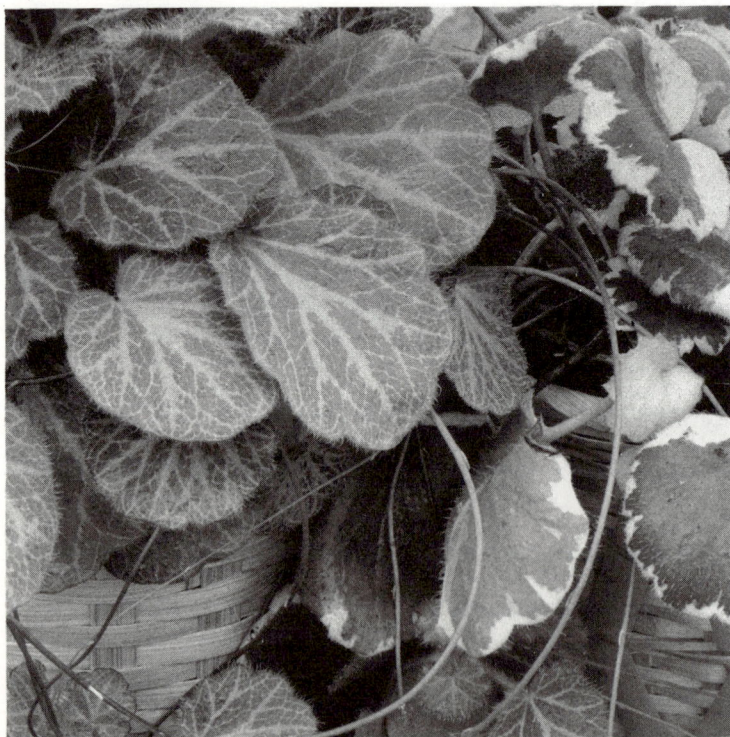

Saxifraga stolonifera Has round grey, green and white striped leaves. The flowers are white. A good basket plant.

Senecio rowleyanus
String of beads

The string of beads is a succulent trailer with small, round light-green leaves and unusual flowers. They are best grown in baskets and kept just moist. *S. heerianus* is closely related and has the same requirements. They grow from cuttings.

See colour plates.

B C E G H   *

Tradescantia
Wandering Jew

The wandering Jew makes a quick hanging basket. They are attractive trailers with variegated foliage that blend well in mixed plantings or alone. Another related wandering Jew is the *Zebrina*. All are hardy and very easy to grow. Regular pruning keeps them bushy. Propagation by cuttings is rapid.

B C F G H K   *

Tradescantia *A number of varieties of Wandering Jew make decorative baskets. Rapid growers needing regular pruning.*

HOUSE PLANT QUICK REFERENCE CHART

CODE KEY

LIGHT LEVELS

A low to medium light levels
B medium to bright filtered light

TEMPERATURE

C cool, minimum 7°C at night
D warm, minimum 15°C at night

WATER REQUIREMENTS

E water thoroughly, allow to dry (not completely) between waterings
F keep evenly moist

SUITABLE ENVIRONMENT

G unheated greenhouse
H permanent indoor growing
J only temporary indoor use
K fernery

BOTANICAL NAME	COMMON NAME	LIGHT		TEMPERATURE		WATERING		SUITABLE ENVIRONMENT			
		A	B	C	D	E	F	G	H	J	K
Achimenes	Hot water plant		■		■		■		■		
Acorus		■		■			■		■		
Adiantum capillus-veneris	Maidenhair fern	■		■			■	■	■		■
Adiantum fragrans	Maidenhair fern		■	■			■	■	■		■
Adiantum hispidulum	Rough maidenhair fern	■	■	■			■	■	■		■
Aeschynanthus	Lipstick plant		■		■	■			■		
Aglaonema	Chinese lucky plant	■			■		■		■		
Anthurium scherzerianum	Flamingo flower		■		■		■		■		
Aphelandra squarrosa	Zebra plant		■		■		■		■		
Ardisia	Coral berry plant		■	■			■	■	■		■
Asparagus	Asparagus fern		■	■			■	■	■		■
Aspidistra	Cast iron plant	■		■			■	■	■		■
Azalea			■	■			■			■	■
Begonia 'Cleopatra'			■		■	■		■	■		
Begonia elatior	Rieger begonia		■		■		■		■		
Begonia rex	Rex begonia		■		■	■		■	■		
Begonia tuberous			■		■		■	■		■	
Boronia			■	■			■		■		
Bougainvillea			■		■		■	■	■		
Bouvardia			■		■		■			■	
Brassaia actinophylla	Umbrella tree		■		■	■			■		
Bromeliads	Vase plants		■	■		■			■		
Browallia			■		■		■		■	■	
Cacti and succulents			■	■		■		■	■	■	■

BOTANICAL NAME	COMMON NAME	LIGHT		TEMPERATURE		WATERING		SUITABLE ENVIRONMENT			
		A	B	C	D	E	F	G	H	J	K
Caladium			■		■		■		■		
Calceolaria			■	■		■		■		■	
Camellia			■	■			■			■	■
Campanula isophylla	Italian bellflower		■	■			■	■		■	■
Ceropegia woodii	Chain of hearts		■	■		■			■		
Chlorophytum	Spider plant	■	■	■			■	■	■		■
Chrysanthemum			■	■			■			■	
Cissus	Grape ivy	■	■		■			■		■	■
Clerodendrum	Bleeding heart vine		■		■		■		■		
Codiaeum	Croton		■		■		■		■		
Coleus			■	■			■	■	■	■	■
Columnea			■		■	■			■		
Cordyline			■		■		■		■		
Crossandra			■		■		■		■		
Cyclamen persicum			■	■			■	■		■	■
Cymbidium	Cymbidium orchid		■	■			■	■		■	
Daphne odora			■	■			■			■	■
Dieffenbachia	Dumb cane		■		■		■		■		
Dizygotheca	Finger aralia		■		■	■			■		
Dracaena			■		■		■		■		
Epipremnum aureus	Devil's ivy	■	■		■	■			■		
Episcia	Flame violet	■			■	■			■		
Erica	Heath		■	■			■			■	
Euphorbia pulcherrima	Poinsettia		■		■	■			■		

161

BOTANICAL NAME	COMMON NAME	LIGHT		TEMPERATURE		WATERING		SUITABLE ENVIRONMENT			
		A	B	C	D	E	F	G	H	J	K
Exacum affine			■		■	■				■	
Fatshedera	Tree aralia	■		■			■	■	■		■
Fatsia	Aralia	■		■			■	■	■		■
Ficus benjamina	Weeping fig		■		■		■		■		■
Ficus pumila	Creeping fig		■	■			■	■	■		■
Ficus radicans	Creeping fig		■	■			■	■	■		■
Fittonia	Nerve plant	■			■		■		■		
Fuchsia			■	■			■	■		■	■
Gardenia			■	■			■			■	■
Geranium			■	■		■		■		■	■
Gibasis	Tahitian bridal veil		■	■			■	■	■		■
Gynura	Velvet plant		■		■		■		■		
Hedera	Ivy	■	■	■			■	■	■	■	■
Helxine	Baby's tears	■		■			■	■	■		■
Hoya	Wax flower		■	■		■		■	■	■	■
Impatiens	Busy lizzie		■		■		■	■		■	■
Ixora			■		■		■		■		
Kalanchoe			■	■		■		■ ,		■	
Lamium	Aluminium creeper	■	■	■			■	■		■	■
Lilium	Lily		■	■			■			■	
Maranta	Prayer plant	■		■			■		■		
Monstera	Fruit salad plant		■	■		■		■	■		■
Nephrolepis varieties			■	■	■	■			■		■
Nephrolepis exaltata 'Bostoniensis'	Boston fern		■	■			■	■	■		■

BOTANICAL NAME	COMMON NAME	LIGHT		TEMPERATURE		WATERING		SUITABLE ENVIRONMENT			
		A	B	C	D	E	F	G	H	J	K
Oplismenus	Rainbow grass		■	■			■	■	■		
Palms		■	■	■	■	■	■	■	■	■	■
Arecastrum romanzoffianum	Cocos plumosa palm	■	■	■			■		■		■
Chamaedorea spp.	Dwarf parlour palms	■	■	■			■		■		■
Chrysalidocarpus lutescens	Golden-cane palm	■	■	■			■		■		■
Howea spp.	Kentia palm	■	■	■			■		■		■
Microcoelum weddeliana	Baby cocos palm	■	■	■			■		■		
Phoenix roebelinii	Pigmy date palm	■	■	■			■		■		■
Rhapis spp.	Lady palm	■	■	■			■		■		■
Peperomia			■		■	■			■		
Philodendron cordatum			■	■			■		■		
Pilea			■		■	■			■		
Plectranthus	Swedish ivy	■	■	■			■	■	■		■
Plumeria	Frangipani		■		■	■		■		■	
Primula	Polyanthus		■	■			■	■		■	■
	Primrose		■	■			■	■		■	■
	P. malacoides		■	■			■	■		■	■
	P. obconica		■	■			■	■		■	■
Pteris	Brake fern	■		■			■	■	■	■	■
Saintpaulia ionantha	African violet		■		■	■			■		
Sansevieria	Snake plant	■	■	■		■			■		
Saxifraga stolonifera	Strawberry begonia		■	■		■		■	■		
Schefflera arboricola	Dwarf umbrella tree		■	■	■		■		■		
Senecio cruentus	Cineraria		■	■		■		■		■	

163

BOTANICAL NAME	COMMON NAME	LIGHT		TEMPERATURE		WATERING		SUITABLE ENVIRONMENT			
		A	B	C	D	E	F	G	H	J	K
Senecio rowleyanus	String of beads		■	■		■		■	■		
Sinningia pusilla	'Doll Baby'		■		■		■		■		
Sinningia speciosa	Gloxinia		■		■		■	■	■		
Spathiphyllum	Madonna lily		■		■		■		■		
Stenochlaena palustris	Qld climbing fern		■	■			■		■		■
Stephanotis			■		■		■		■		
Streptocarpus	Cape primrose		■	■			■		■		
Syngonium	Goosefoot	■	■	■			■		■		
Tolmeia	Piggy-back plant	■		■			■	■	■		■
Tradescantia	Wandering Jew		■	■			■	■	■		■

Part 3

SPECIALTY PLANTINGS AND EXTENDING OUTDOORS

HANGING
BASKETS

———

HANGING BASKETS are handy where there is a shortage of space and show many plants to a better advantage than standard pots. One such is the trailing fuchsia, a superb flowering pot plant which is outstanding as a basket specimen. The natural habit of the plant is encouraged and the full beauty of form and flower can be appreciated.

Hanging baskets can be used in the home for interior decoration, in the transition between garden and house, or in greenhouses and ferneries. The aesthetic value of the basket to the plant and the surroundings is important and may be somewhat diminished if the colour of the basket clashes with those of the plant and the decor. Out of doors this is not as noticeable but, if the plant is the focus, the basket should be relatively unobtrusive.

Greenery is well suited to basket culture, and the familiar favourites of boston fern, elk and stag ferns, and ivies thrive in all but the coldest localities. Sensitive varieties demand extra care during frosty periods.

The wire basket lined with fibre or sphagnum moss is very attractive, yet quite impractical for interior decoration. There are obvious problems of thorough watering and preventing drips spoiling valuable carpets and furnishings. Thus it is out of doors where the wire basket comes into its own. By combining suitable lining materials such as sphagnum and bush moss with a dash of imagination, the entire surface can be planted giving an outstanding result. Trailing annuals and perennials carefully blended in this way will add brightness to porches and patios throughout the year.

The plastic basket with the clip-on saucer facilitates easier watering and provides a useful reserve of moisture during hot periods. A well-designed basket has a flat-

The ready-shaped coconut-fibre liners are ideal for lining a wire basket. Secure the hangers with pliers.

bottomed saucer which sits squarely on any level surface. Thus with the hangers removed, the basket doubles as a pot.

INDOOR BASKETS

Plants growing in baskets have similar cultural requirements to those grown in pots. There are some pitfalls in the areas of light, heat and moisture that warrant attention. Unfortunately out of sight is out of mind, and with baskets close to the ceiling it is easy to overlook their needs. Watering is rarely effective unless the basket is taken down and treated as a normal pot. Allow the soil to drain completely and empty the saucer before replacing the basket.

The difference in temperature between the floor and ceiling is often significant enough to cause ordinarily hardy varieties to fail. All plants grown indoors in hanging baskets must be both tolerant of heat and stuffiness and to poor light. The thick waxy foliage of *Philodendron cordatum* and *Epipremnum aureum* (Devil's ivy) makes them ideal.

Remember that a fully grown basket is surprisingly heavy and capable of creating havoc unless adequately secured with chains and hooks of sufficient strength.

Trim the sphagnum moss around the basket to improve the effect. Note that the moss extends well beyond the wire lip.

OUTDOOR BASKETS

Plastic baskets are equally suited to outdoor and indoor uses. More moisture is retained, which is an asset in hot weather. But as a precaution against waterlogging in winter, the saucers should be removed to encourage free drainage of surplus water.

The materials for lining wire baskets include moss, paperbark, seaweed, coconut fibre and the synthetic fibres. The liner serves the dual role of improving the overall appearance and retaining the potting mix. For speedy potting, the pre-shaped coconut fibre liners are convenient and generally last longer than moss, paper-bark and seaweed. Lining with the loose materials is satisfying, but can be frustrating at times. An even and adequate thickness is essential to prevent soil loss and rapid dehydration. The materials are easier to work with if dampened thoroughly beforehand. An internal lining of plastic with drainage holes *cut* out will help water retention.

Before planting-up, firm the potting mix into the base and sides. Leave enough room at the top for watering, and on no account fill the basket to the rim with mixture. The lining material should always be at least 2 to 5 cm higher than the soil level after watering and settling. Some additional peatmoss worked into the mix is particularly valuable in retaining extra moisture.

Summer winds and heat are the bane of the basket grower, and on hot days twice daily watering may be necessary. Hot drying winds damage even the toughest plants and, wherever practical, it is advisable to relocate baskets to a protected area.

The installation of drip and spray systems linked to automatic or manual time-clocks can certainly simplify watering. The systems can be programmed to accommodate the prevailing conditions and are a godsend for the summer vacationer. They use water more effectively and can be set to operate during off-peak when the pressure is best. The best time to water is in the early hours before sunrise. During especially hot weather though, time clocks can be programmed to water the baskets during the day.

TYPES OF BASKETS

Plastic and wire baskets come in a range of styles, qualities and prices. The thinner the plastic, the quicker it heats up and usually the shorter the basket's life.

The hanger that clips onto the lip of the plastic basket is easier to remove but not as secure as one that pushes into a slot. Avoid very thin hangers which can break if bent. The saucer should attach and detach easily and stay firmly in place when knocked or full of water.

The plastic-coated wire basket lasts considerably longer than the standard galvanized type. Price largely reflects the quality of wire (gauge) and the method of fabrication. Spot welding of each junction lends added strength and prevents distortion. Some types use tie-wire instead of welds. Any basket which bends readily while empty may well pull out of shape when planted.

PLANTING

Wire baskets
Choose a basket with enough volume to suit the plant. Allow for loss of volume taken by the liner. Sit the basket in an upturned pot for ease of work, and add the liner. Firm the potting mix around the sides and base. Centre the plant, add the mix and firm lightly. Water well; top up with extra mix as needed. Attach the hangers. Hang the basket and trim away any untidy pieces of liner.

Plastic baskets
Potting-up a plastic basket is no different to an ordinary container. It is much easier to attach the saucer before you fill the basket with mix. Once the planting is satisfactorily completed, secure and test the hangers. Water thoroughly and empty the excess water out of the saucer before lifting the basket into place.

BASKET CARE

Plants grown in baskets require the routine tasks of pruning, feeding, repotting and pest control. Fast-growing plants, including the colourful annuals, need yearly repotting. If a good quality planting mix is used initially, and regular feeding carried out, annual repotting of established baskets is not necessary.

PLANTS FOR HANGING BASKETS

THOSE HOUSE plants commonly used in hanging baskets are listed in alphabetical order of botanical names. The list shows whether they are mainly grown for their flowers or for their foliage, as well as the most suitable environment in which to grow them.

CODE KEY

G unheated greenhouse

H permanent indoor growing

J only temporary indoor use

K fernery

BOTANICAL NAME	COMMON NAME	FLOWERS	FOLIAGE	SUITABLE ENVIRONMENT			
				G	H	J	K
Achimenes	Hot water plant	■			■		
Aeschynanthus	Lipstick plant	■	■		■		
Asparagus spp.	Asparagus fern		■	■	■		■
Azalea		■				■	■
Begonia spp.		■		■	■	■	
Camellia (selected varieties)		■				■	■
Ceropegia woodii	Chain of hearts	■	■		■		
Chlorophytum	Spider plant		■	■	■		■
Cissus	Grape ivy		■		■		■
Clerodendrum	Bleeding heart vine	■			■		
Coleus			■	■	■	■	■
Columnea		■	■		■		
Epipremnum aureus	Devil's ivy		■		■		
Episcia	Flame violet	■	■		■		
Ferns			■	■	■		■
Ficus pumila, F. radicans	Creeping fig		■	■	■		■
Fuchsia		■			■	■	■
Gardenia		■				■	■
Geranium		■				■	■
Gibasis	Tahitian bridal veil	■	■	■	■		■
Gynura	Velvet plant		■		■		
Hedera	Ivy		■	■	■		■
Helxine	Baby's tears		■	■	■		■

BOTANICAL NAME	COMMON NAME	FLOWERS	FOLIAGE	SUITABLE ENVIRONMENT			
				G	H	J	K
Hoya	Wax flower	■		■	■	■	■
Impatiens	Busy lizzie	■	■	■		■	■
Kalanchoe		■		■		■	
Lamium	Aluminium creeper		■	■	■		■
Maranta	Prayer plant		■		■		
Oplismenus	Rainbow grass		■	■	■		
Peperomia			■		■		
Philodendron spp.			■		■		
Pilea			■		■		
Plectranthus	Swedish ivy		■	■	■		■
Saintpaulia (trailers)	African violet	■			■		
Saxifraga stolonifera	Strawberry begonia	■	■	■	■		■
Senecio rowleyanus	String of beads	■	■	■	■		
Streptocarpus	Cape primrose	■			■		
Syngonium	Goosefoot		■		■		
Tolmeia	Piggy-back plant		■	■	■		■
Tradescantia	Wandering Jew		■	■	■		■
Annuals for seasonal colour		■	■	■		■	■

TERRARIUMS AND BOTTLE GARDENS

TERRARIUMS OR bottle gardens provide excellent growing conditions for many tropical plants in situations where they otherwise would have failed. The terrarium combines the essential growth factors into a confined package that demands little grower input. Watering is greatly reduced, relying upon recirculated condensation when the container is airtight, or infrequent topping up if it is open to the air. An excess of water is the commonest source of failure.

The growing medium of a terrarium comprises three layers of material. A generous layer of charcoal at the base to keep the soil sweet; next some sphagnum moss to retain and absorb moisture; and finally the potting mixture. Only minimal quantities of fertilizer are added to the potting mix because high levels force extravagant growth and create problems for plant health. Additional food is applied by a few prills of a slow-release fertilizer.

Perhaps an unused fishtank sits in your garage now that the initial attraction has waned. It is ideal for use as a terrarium, and infinitely more practical than a bottle. Access for routine maintenance is straightforward, thus any corrective action does not require a major upheaval.

The basic rectangular shape is less restrictive in designing a layout. The attractive multi-angled shapes using reflective glass allow you to design interesting landscapes. Bear in mind that flowering plants need greater care than foliage plants because the dead blooms rot rapidly if left in place.

The terrarium is like a miniature greenhouse, having high humidity and warmth. The potential for rampant fungal growth is enormous and a few minutes per week to remove spent flowers and leaves is recommended.

Plants such as asparagus, gynura, plectranthus and the tradescantias are unsuitable because their already vigorous growth is further stimulated by the warmth and humidity of the terrarium.

But terrariums must never sit in direct sunlight. The rays are concentrated by the glass and very few plants can survive a pressure cooking for long. If an old aquarium is used and the fluorescent fitting is operable, you can grow plants successfully using only artificial light.

Suitable plants are shown in the table, though some are suited only for larger containers.

Plants suited for growing in terrariums or bottle gardens

Acorus	*Ficus pumila*
Adiantum capillus-veneris	*Ficus radicans* **variegata**
Adiantum fragrans	*Fittonia*
Adiantum hispidulum	*Hedera*
Aeschynanthus	*Helxine*
Aglaonema	*Maranta*
Anthurium	*Microcoelum weddeliana*
Aphelandra	*Peperomia*
Begonia **'Cleopatra'** **types**	*Pilea*
	Pteris
Begonia rex	*Saintpaulia*
Bromeliads **(*Cryptanthus*, etc.)**	*Sansevieria trifasciata* **'Hahnii'**
Chamaedorea elegans	*Sansevieria trifasciata* **'Laurentii'**
Codiaeum	
Cordyline	*Saxifraga sarmentosa*
Dracaena	*Sinningia pusilla*
Epipremnum	**'Doll Baby'**

GREENHOUSES

TRADITIONALLY THE glasshouse utilized glass as the cladding material, thus the name. Nowadays the term greenhouse is preferable because cladding materials include plastic films, acrylic and polycarbonate sheeting, and fibreglass. All materials used have two properties in common, they transmit the light and the heat both necessary for good growth. These modern materials have given a new approach to greenhouse structure and operation; the elasticity of the plastic film giving a degree of freedom previously unavailable. The igloo or tunnel is a cheap alternative to the solid glasshouse-type structure which must be perfectly square and strong enough to accommodate the rigidity and weight of the glass. Fibreglass and similar non-vitreous sheet products are much lighter and easier to install and for this reason more practical for the home gardener.

FRAME

The prices for basic kit greenhouses reflect the structural, cladding and benching materials used, with extras to suit. A careful comparison between the models offered is necessary. A flimsy structure in a windy location is foolish and, similarly, a fortress in protected areas is a waste of resources. Local councils have regulations governing these buildings and a visit beforehand will save money and effort later on. The basic framework of the greenhouse is the most important part because the overall life and safety depend upon it. Whenever possible galvanized steel or aluminium are preferred to timber which rots and requires more maintenance.

CLADDING

Cladding alternatives dictate the style of construction. They are rated according to expected life and ability to transmit light (which usually declines with age). Glass has the longest life and the highest light transmission. Fibreglass, polythene and acrylic twin-walled sheets all deteriorate at different rates due to the ultraviolet rays from the sun. Fibreglass in particular can have very poor light transmission depending upon the colour of the dye, for example blue, green and yellow let in less sunlight than clear or white. Naturally, the better the quality (including thickness), the dearer the product.

Polythene films are the cheapest of all for home use and have the distinct advantage of needing a lightweight construction. The film is pliable and will mould to the shape of the supports so that a slightly off-square frame is easily accommodated. These plastic films are available in various thicknesses, with or without an ultraviolet inhibitor, with some incorporating fibre tougheners. A bubble version gives extra insulation. The life span can be quite short in areas of high sunlight and strong winds. It pays to buy the best at the outset. Regular replacement is necessary and this is undoubtedly the major disincentive to their use. The polythene films give excellent light transmission.

SITING

Light is the major consideration when siting the greenhouse, although the site is often determined by existing uses of the backyard. Light levels become critical during the grey and sunless winter periods, consequently greenhouses positioned to capture maximum light at this time give excellent results, while those permanently shaded by evergreen trees often fail. High shade from trees in summer is advantageous, helping to lessen the amount of artificial shading required.

INTERIOR

Once the exterior of the greenhouse is determined, the interior requires some thought. A concrete floor is perfect for cleanliness, but may not be to your taste or budget. Packed earth is unadvisable as it acts as a haven for slugs, and tends to become wet and slippery. Blue metal and crushed scoria drain well and are relatively cheap.

Benching makes life a lot easier and is essential for maintaining healthy stock. All-metal benches resist decay and those with mesh tops promote air circulation and speed up drainage of waste water. Tiered benching utilizes space efficiently and means better use of differing light levels. Plants raised above a cold floor have warmer soil and roots, and are less likely to pick up fungal diseases.

HEATING

There is no disputing the addition of a heater to a greenhouse is rewarding. Growth is enhanced and the variety of suitable house plants cultivated is noticeably larger. The biggest factor contributing to the death of most exotics during winter is cold, wet soil rather than poor light or even cool air temperatures. Thus a heater means warmer soil and all the benefits that accrue. Electric fan heaters are especially effective for circulating warmed air and they operate thermostatically. Gas-fired units are costlier to install but equally as good. It is worthwhile contacting your local energy authorities for comparative estimates of running costs using their product before choosing a heating system. Any system which burns fuel to produce heat also produces flue gases. These are harmful to plants and must be ventilated to the outside by an approved flue pipe.

Not everyone wants or can afford heating. The cold greenhouse is just as satisfying, although the type of plant is different. Cymbidium orchids, cineraria, *Primula*, many fern species, *Cyclamen* and *Kalanchoe* (to name a few) are suited only to cool growing. Frosty regions are a problem, and some protection for the cool growing varieties may be needed occasionally.

VENTILATION AND SHADING

Excess heat stresses the plant and stops growth. Scorching and death will result without adequate ventilation. The smaller the structure, the faster it heats up and cools down. Allowance for ventilators at roof level is mandatory, with extra side ventilators as necessary.

Shade cloth and shading compounds reduce the light

and hence the heat entering the greenhouse. Few plants can withstand bright unfiltered light without damage. Shade cloth is manufactured in specified degrees of shade, while the spray-on materials are diluted accordingly.

For ease of application, a framework built over a greenhouse, to which the cloth is tied, is ideal. The newer, knotted cloths do not fray if damaged accidentally.

Spray-on shade is cheaper but messy. Thorough mixing is essential for even coverage, and a reasonable sense of humour to deal with blocked nozzles. The timing for applying and removing any shading is a balancing act between the usual seasonal conditions and freak sunny and dull spells; one day's misjudgement can destroy months of work.

SOME TIPS

Some tips when using the greenhouse include:
- segregate cold- and heat-loving species;
- use light levels to advantage;
- keep pots off the ground;
- water in the early morning during the cooler months;
- moderate temperatures, for example 15°C, keep most exotics in good health, and fuel costs down;
- pests and diseases love protected environments, so take care;
- in winter segregate plants preferring infrequent watering;
- never throw rubbish, pots or soil under benches;
- remove all dead plant matter regularly.

FERNERIES

THE COOL-CLIMATE fernery provides the protected environment to grow a range of cool and temperate growing species quite successfully. The real tropicals rarely survive, however among the ferns there are those such as the boston fern, bird's nest fern, and elkhorn fern (*Platycerium*) which have adapted to the cold winters.

A fernery need not be restricted exclusively to ferns, but enlarged to include plants for which no suitable aspect exists in the garden. Azaleas, camellias and rhododendrons appreciate the shade and humidity, as do fuchsias, impatiens, cineraria, coleus and cyclamen.

Frost and cold winds can cause severe damage even to the best protected fernery. Sensitive plants should be moved to warmer areas or protected by hessian whenever frost is imminent.

Summertime contains a few traps to the unwary, the most common being underwatering. Shade-cloth materials certainly lower the intensity of the sunlight, but do not reduce the temperature sufficiently to decrease water use by the plant. Poorly ventilated ferneries located in such a way as to trap summer heat are detrimental to plant health. It is possible to lose a plant, even though the soil is wet, because of hot, stuffy air. Similarly, a pocket of icy air can be trapped in a poorly-ventilated fernery.

The successful fernery combines good air circulation without hot and cold winds, and draughts. Once solid walls are introduced, eliminating draughts is important. An area at the top of each solid wall is covered-in with shade cloth to encourage venting of hot air. These vents are readily covered with plastic sheeting during winter, however some general air circulation is essential at all times.

If a waterproof roof is desired, fibreglass sheeting is easy to install and is lightweight. Rain can be a nuisance by spoiling delicate blooms and foliage. Damp foliage tends to encourage fungi and continually wet soil is to be avoided. (Remove all saucers from plastic buckets prior to winter to prevent waterlogging.) Special care is imperative once the days heat up wherever fibreglass is used for roofing and on exposed walls. It is a hot material, and those plants in contact or within close proximity (say 30 cm) on a hot day without shading invariably burn. Shade by itself is not enough; the hot air must be able to escape.

Structurally, flat-roofed designs are preferred, with allowance for drainage wherever rainproof cladding is used. Benching, flooring and framework considerations are similar to the greenhouse. A porous floor holds added moisture for summertime humidification and doesn't become slippery. The shade-cloth materials come in differing percentages of shade to suit the plants to be cultivated. If the shading requirements alter, a second layer can be added. Some growers attach this secondary shading to timber frames which are located as necessary. Each manufacturer has specific recommendations on attaching shade cloth to the framework. Follow these exactly.

The landscaped fernery with permanent plantings is most attractive. A keen eye for design and creative planting will result in a delightful setting. A sprinkler system is particularly advantageous for permanent plantings. The sprinkler kits are straightforward and fast to install. The special dripper outlets make watering of hanging baskets and pots easy. The whole system is readily automated with low-cost time-clocks so that the problem of holiday watering disappears.

Slugs, snails, earwigs and slaters delight in the moisture of a fernery and the ready source of food it offers. Routine removal of spent foliage and flowers together with judicious use of poison baits help lessen the damage. Any reduction in the hiding places afforded by empty pots and accumulated debris is helpful. Grubs and caterpillars are troublesome at any time of the year, and may do substantial damage during the cooler months if routine maintenance is neglected.

Hanging baskets are remarkably heavy when the plant is fully grown and the soil moist. The framework should be sturdy enough to carry these with a sufficient margin of safety. Set the uprights in a solid and ample foundation of concrete, with crossbeams and bracing of adequate strength. Most local councils have building regulations to control such structures. Consult with the local building inspector prior to building and obtain the necessary permits.

Index of botanical names

Index of common names

Saintpaulia ionantha, 11, 48, **67–9**, 97, 163, 174, 176
Sanseviera, 7, 8, 48, **155–6**, 163, 176
Saxifraga stolonifera, 48, **156**, 163, 174, 176
Schefflera arboricola, 48, **131–2**, 163
Senecio cruentus, 48, **93**, 97, 163
— rowleyanus, 49, **157**, 164, 174
Sinningia pusilla, 49, **94**, 97, 164, 176
— speciosa, 49, 70, 97, 164
Spathiphyllum, 49, **71–2**, 97, 164
Stenochlaena palustris, 49, **132–4**, 164
Stephanotis, 49, **94**, 97, 164
Streptocarpus, 49, **72–4**, 97, 164, 174
Syngonium, 26, 49, **134–6**, 164, 174

Tolmeia menziesii, 7, 8, 49, **137–8**, 164, 174
Tradescantia, 49, **157**, 164, 174

African violet, 5, 13, 25, 40, 48, **67–9**, 97, 163, 174
Aluminium creeper, 47, **150–1**, 162, 174
Aralia, 47, **147**, 162
Asparagus fern, 45, **141**, 160, 173

Baby Cocos palm, 48, **151**, 163
Baby's tears, 47, **150**, 162, 173
Balsam, **63–5**
Bleeding Heart vine, 46, **83–4**, 96, 161, 173
Boston ferns, 47, 121, **124–5**, 162, 167
Brake fern, 48, **154–5**, 163
Brown boronia, **77**, 96
Busy Lizzie, 47, **63–5**, 97, 162, 174

Cape primrose, 49, **72–4**, 97, 164, 174
Cast iron plant, 45, **142**, 160
Chain of hearts, 46, **144–5**, 161, 173
Chinese lucky plant, 4, 45, **102–3**, 160
Cineraria, 4, 48, **93**, 97, 163, 179, 181
Cocos plumosa palm, 48, 125, 163
Coral berry plant, 45, **141**, 160
Creeping fig, 47, **116–18**, 162, 173
Croton, 4, 25, 46, **105–6**, 161

Devil's Ivy, 46, **111–12**, 161, 168, 173
Doll Baby, 49, **94**, 97, 164
Dumb cane, 46, **106–7**, 161
Dwarf parlour palm, 48, 126, 163
Dwarf umbrella plant, 48, **131–2**, 163

Ferns, 31, 173, 179, 181
Finger aralia, 46, **108–9**, 161
Fishbone ferns, 41, 121

Flame violet, 46, **86**, 96, 161, 173
Flamingo flower, 45, **55–6**, 96, 160
Frangipani, 48, **92–3**, 97, 163
Fruit salad plant, 47, **152**, 162

Gloxinia, 49, **70–1**, 97, 164
Golden cane palm, 48, 127, 163
Goosefoot, 49, 164, 174
Grape Ivy, 26, 46, **104–5**, 161, 173

Heath, 46, **87**, 97, 161
Hotwater plant, 45, **75**, 96, 160, 173

Italian bellflower, 46, **82**, 96, 120
Ivy, 25, 47, **149**, 162, 173

Kentia palm, 5, 48, 125, 163

Lady palm, 48, 125, 127, 163
Lily, 47, **92**, 97, 162
Lipstick plant, 45, **53–4**, 96, 160, 173

Madonna lily, 49, **71–2**, 97, 164
Maidenhair ferns, 4, 45, **99–102**, **140**, 160

Nerve plant, 47, **148**, 162

Piggyback plant, 7, 8, 10, 15, 49, **137–8**, 164, 174
Pigmy date palm, 46, 126, 163
Poinsettia, 5, 46, **62–3**, 97, 161
Polyanthus, 4, 48, **65–7**, 97, 163
Prayer plant, 47, **119–21**, 162, 174
Primrose, 48, **65–7**, 97, 163

185